"*Growing Groups into Teams* is an impo. ...., too. This is the guide so many teams have needed. Working with Altus truly makes a difference, and this book lays the groundwork for making teams of all kinds more successful."

TIM MOORE, *CTO, Allogene Therapeutics*

"*Growing Groups into Teams* is a must-read for groups that want to transform into amazing teams that produce results and energize members. With its practical guidance, real-life examples, and actionable strategies, this book is a valuable resource for anyone looking to build a high-performance team."

LAURA FRANCIS, *CEO, SI-BONE, Inc.*

"A must-read for leaders at all levels. I highly recommend *Growing Groups into Teams* for your entire organization."

AKE PERSSON, *Former CEO, Ericsson North America*

"*Growing Groups into Teams* arrived at the right time for me. The practical advice and real-life examples offered in the book helped me understand underlying issues and gave me concrete steps to take to improve our situation. I recommend this book for every company and organization at the growth stage who may be wondering why they're not getting the results they expect—despite hiring more people."

CONGYU LI, *CTO & co-founder, StoreHub*

"The future of work is built on great teams. Understanding how to better create, mobilize, and leverage teams will not help us to get more done, it will make work better."

MEG BEAR, *President & Chief Product Officer, SAP SuccessFactors*

"Our health system has been working collaboratively with Altus over the past two years, and we have literally transformed from a leadership committee to an effective executive leadership team. The practice and coaching described in *Growing Groups into Teams* is so impactful. We are now leading by exceptionally team-oriented results, delivering a sustainable future for our organization."

MAGGIE HUDSON, *CEO, Santiam Hospital & Clinics*

"This book moves the thinking and practice of building high performing and inclusive teams forward with insightful perspective that's much needed as we set higher and higher expectations for business performance."

SUSAN WHITEHEAD, *President & COO, PACT Pharma*

"Finally. A book about teams written by a diverse team of authors. How refreshing to find a book that is inclusive of different types of organizations and cultures."

RONDA JACKSON, *Vice President Policy, Advocacy, and Impact, KABOOM!*

"Altus has helped us tune our teams for high performance. I'm glad to see they're sharing their expertise on this subject more broadly. *Growing Groups into Teams* will be a valuable resource for groups throughout your organization."

PAYMON HAMIDI, *CEO, Infracore*

"When I work with organizations to launch new subscription or membership initiatives, strong teams are critical. This book sharpened my thinking about how to build them!"

ROBBIE KELLMAN BAXTER, *Author of* The Membership Economy *and* The Forever Transaction

"As a trusted provider of consulting and interim staffing in high tech, government, and healthcare, our people must integrate quickly and effectively into existing and new teams to deliver unprecedented results. This book shows us what to look at on teams to make them even more successful."

NITI AGRAWAL, *CEO, Stage 4 Solutions*

"This book takes time to measure the success of teams from the lens of both business and sports. *Growing Groups into Teams* clarifies the difference between groups and teams and the lack of the success that groups have because they are not teams. Whether you're in a start-up, turn-around, or reorganization, the tools provided will guide you and your team toward the shared values and mission that will yield the results for which your organization was established. *Growing Groups into Teams* provides a template that any organization can implement to prevent those failures and allows leaders to create a culture of trust."

FLOYD AKINS, *Vice President for Advancement, University of Toledo*

GROWING GROUPS INTO TEAMS

Real-life stories of people who get
results and thrive together

KOBE BOGAERT
PAM FOX ROLLIN
and the Team at
ALTUS GROWTH PARTNERS

Altus Leadership Press

Published by Altus Leadership Press

www.altusgrowth.com

LIBRARY OF CONGRESS CATALOGING-IN-PUBLICATION DATA

Names: Bogaert, Kobe, author. | Fox Rollin, Pam, author. | Altus Growth Partners, sponsoring body.

Title: Growing groups into teams : real-life stories of people who get results and thrive together / Kobe Bogaert, Pam Fox Rollin and the team at Altus Growth Partners.

Description: [San Diego, California] : Altus Leadership Press, [2023] | Includes bibliographical references and index.

Identifiers: ISBN: 979-8-9889595-0-2 (hardback) | 979-8-9889595-1-9 (paperback) | 979-8-9889595-2-6 (ebook)

Subjects: LCSH: Teams in the workplace. | Teams in the workplace--Management. | Teams in the workplace--Training of. | Transformational leadership. | Cooperativeness. | Trust. | Industrial management. | Management--Employee participation. | Work ethic. | Work environment. | Leadership. | BISAC: BUSINESS & ECONOMICS / Leadership. | BUSINESS & ECONOMICS / Workplace Culture.

Classification: LCC: HD66 .B64 2023 | DDC: 658.4/022--dc23

*"If you want to go fast,
go alone.
If you want to go far,
go together."*

-Proverb of disputed origin

We dedicate this book to you, the reader,

who wants a better future for yourself,

your teammates, and those who benefit

from what you produce together.

TABLE OF CONTENTS

FOREWORD

In May 2019, Ken Blanchard and I published *Helping People Win at Work*, which gave us the opportunity to share the experiences of WD-40 Company in helping people succeed. So, when Kobe Bogaert asked me to write the foreword for this book, I was excited to hear that he and his team are sharing their experiences on how to build, grow, and nourish teams.

This is an important subject for me as a leader, as it is my mission in life to help other leaders find a better way to create thriving companies, enlivened by dedicated, talented people who come to work every day with one mission in mind: To make life better at work and at home. And when they come home, their happiness and sense of fulfillment serve as an inspiring example to their children—who will one day grow up and experience their own satisfying work life and serve as inspiring role models for generations to come.

I'm aware that there are many CEOs who solely focus on results without paying attention to the concerns of their people. Gallup Research has found that 69% of the workforce in the US is not engaged or actively disengaged.[1] In many organizations, it's not unusual to see people struggle with collaboration and working together effectively. People dread going to work, and they feel depleted when they come home. Gallup calculates that disengagement costs the economy about 9% of GDP every year[2], and it's the cause of illnesses, bad attitudes at home, and even wrecked families.

I see that many organizations reward individual performance rather than what they accomplish as a team. Often this comes with a singular focus on a few results, without paying attention to why and how those results are produced. They make decisions to create short-term wins, but ignore long-term problems. They're not building strong relationships, and there's more distrust than collective success. Obviously, nobody designs their organization to be that way—it's just how things end up, because building a great team isn't always obvious.

It doesn't have to be that way. We designed WD-40 Company and built a culture where teams operate in ways that support each individual. This is a place where people are energized by the work and connection that they have with each other. It's where they make contributions to things bigger than themselves, where they are constantly learning, and as a result, go home happy and fulfilled.

As CEO of WD-40 Company, I realize that leadership is a 24/7, 365-day-a-year contact sport. Leadership is not about you. It's not about being in charge—it's about taking care of those in your charge.[3] As a leader, I'm responsible for creating an environment that allows people go to work every day and make their best contributions.

I can't do this by myself. We look for team members who are both high performers and values-driven players. In our culture, every leader is responsible to help and coach their team members to get an A. We cultivate learning and teaching, which produces a highly engaged workforce who live our company's values every day.

For every team, we plan for what success looks like every year. This requires that we consistently review with caring and candor what we are doing, how we are succeeding, and obstacles that might be in the way. Open communication is a must for our culture at WD-40 Company, as a place where people belong. In our company, we don't make mistakes, we have learning moments. This is also what Kobe and his team show you how to create in this book.

That's why I'm excited about the experiences shared in this book. I find them relevant for anyone who wants to be successful in building and leading amazing teams. The authors share why it's important to build teams that can withstand the test of time in today's complex global, virtual, and 'always on' environment. I appreciate how they explore the promises we also make to grow into a great team and how to set your team up to thrive in a diverse world.

Each chapter explores what it takes to build great teams in different real-life situations. At the same time, this book reveals the pitfalls in which we often find ourselves—and how to move through them with dignity and mutual respect.

There are many books that describe what a team looks like but darn few that share actual experiences of how to go about building teams to be successful together. I trust you'll enjoy reading this book as much as I did and use what you learn to make your teams even more successful.

G'day and have fun!

Garry Ridge
Chairman Emeritus
WD-40 Company

WELCOME

To Build a Better Future, Build a Better Team

Kobe Bogaert and Pam Fox Rollin

Companies and organizations accomplish much of their work in teams, and the effectiveness of these teams powers results. The experience of working within teams impacts how long people stay and how well people innovate and collaborate to drive the next round of success. Whether you are a team member, leader, investor, customer, or community member, much of your happiness, health, and wealth depends on the success of teams.

---

*Much of your happiness, health, and
wealth depends on the success of teams.*

Let's say you have an amazing team.

Your team achieves and surpasses the results that matter to customers and the company. Most days, people are energized to work and feel satisfied, rather than drained. Team members communicate with honesty and respect, make promises that customers and other teams trust, and adapt readily to changing constraints and opportunities.

Joining your team might be a goal for others in the company or industry. It may even become one of the most rewarding parts of daily life for your team members. When team members are promoted or leave to start a company, they'll want to make their new teams as successful as yours. Your main fear, if any, when you're on an amazing team, is that the good times will come to an end, and you're uncertain on how to repeat this success.

Some teams are "just OK."

People on these teams work hard, come up with good ideas, diligently slay task lists, reorder those lists as priorities change, and do their best to get along. The work mostly gets done, other departments don't often complain, and everyone has a relatively decent day most of the time.

Yet, team members know something is missing. It's the sense that we're in this together—the eagerness to surmount challenges, the support for each other's efforts and growth, the determination to drive more value, and the shared discipline to make it so.

It's just so hard to name exactly what's not there.

While we all want amazing teams, most organizations tolerate many teams that are not.

If you only had that X factor—that clear direction or good mojo—you suspect the interactions with this team would feel even better, and the team would be making a bigger difference to the future of your careers, the company, and your customers.

Then there are the teams that people avoid.

Maybe this team isn't making its numbers. Maybe the most capable team members leave as soon as they can, and it's difficult to attract replacements. Maybe other functions—or even customers—avoid working with this team. Maybe team members find it hard to drag themselves to their computers each morning, and they know that others feel the same way.

You look at this team and see handoffs botched, information hoarded, and energy wasted on projects that never earn the full support of the team. Some people on the team don't even talk to each other anymore. If you've parachuted into this team as a leader or team member, you wonder whether you have what it takes to turn this around. You wonder if that's even possible.

While we all want amazing teams, most organizations tolerate many teams that are not.

Sixty-five percent of companies in Deloitte's Global Human Capital Trends viewed the shift to team-based models as important for high performance, yet only 6% rated their company as effective in managing cross-functional teams.[4] *Training* magazine and Ken Blanchard Companies found that only 27% of employees and managers said their teams performed at optimum levels even half of the time.[5]

Many mediocre "teams" aren't actually teams. They're groups of task-doers.

We tend to assume performance is a natural consequence of working in a group. Yet, a group of great people doesn't automatically accomplish great results that meet the needs of internal and external customers. When people work in a group, each person has their own set of tasks, and they're focused on doing their own work. When we shift to becoming a team, it's the team performance that counts.

Let's look at the defining differences between groups and teams:

GROUPS	TEAMS
• Do work that relates in some way	• Commit to a shared promise
• Defined by reporting structure	• Defined by their shared promise
• Rewarded for their individual tasks	• Rewarded for their contribution to fulfilling the shared promise
• Members avoid bothering each other	• Members actively support each other
• Leadership defines targets, allocates tasks, and reviews performance[6]	• Leadership grows and mentors the team to make and fulfill ever more valuable promises

These differences mean groups create more miscues and miscoordination, experience conflict avoidance and self-promoting behavior, resort to finger pointing, and—unsurprisingly—underperform. Teams, as defined above, tend to accomplish and innovate more, understand their customers better, actively engage diverse perspectives and skills, learn faster, provide more professional development and satisfaction, and adapt faster to changing circumstances.

An amazing team is one that makes a shared promise with observable outcomes, navigates challenges together, and creates valuable results, with each team member supported.

Of course, you don't get the benefits of teams for free. Building, developing, and sustaining teams takes skill and commitment. Teams take more time to align, build trust, and coordinate well, yet this time pays off in smoother implementation and more valuable innovation.

When do you need a team, rather than a group of task-doers?

- When you're aiming to do things the organization hasn't done before, as teams provide diverse expertise and crucial psychological safety for experimenting and learning.
- When people can accomplish their objectives only with input and help, as teams encourage mutual support.
- When your team must influence and partner with others in the company, as teams enable crucial alignment and coordination.
- When customers want a substantially new product or experience, as team members share the commitment needed to overcome roadblocks, align on a specific future, and coordinate their actions to build it.

We say that an amazing team is one that makes a shared promise with observable outcomes, navigates challenges together, and creates valuable results, with each team member supported to grow in this team or the next.

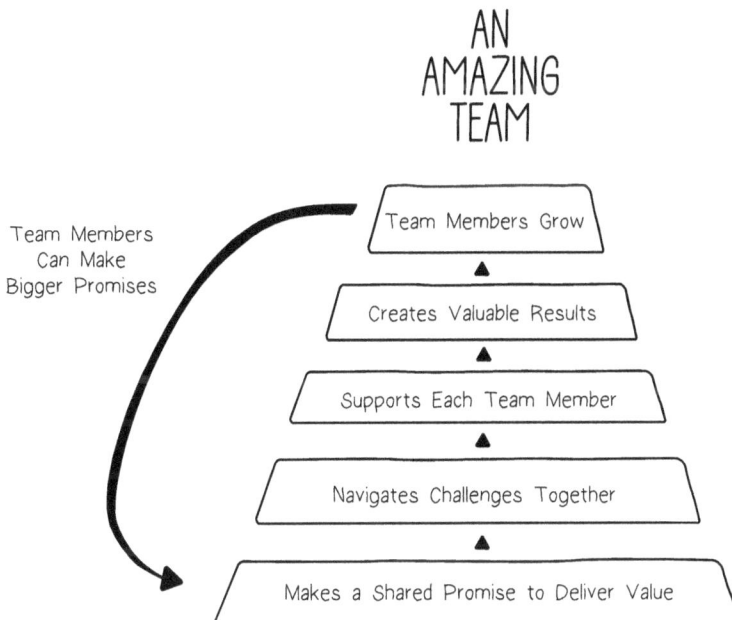

AN AMAZING TEAM

Team Members Can Make Bigger Promises

Team Members Grow

▲

Creates Valuable Results

▲

Supports Each Team Member

▲

Navigates Challenges Together

▲

Makes a Shared Promise to Deliver Value

Every group has the potential to become an amazing team.

In our work at Altus Growth Partners, we've helped companies, governments, and NGOs around the world succeed in creating amazing teams that produce results that matter and energize their members—even when the work is hard and the circumstances challenging. We've strengthened senior teams in Los Angeles, London, Boston, Bangalore, Barcelona, Toronto, Beijing, Sao Paolo, Kuala Lumpur, and many other places. We've led Silicon Valley software teams, rust belt manufacturing turnarounds, and nonprofit mergers. We've guided community initiatives from Zambia to Panama to Australia to bring forward their diversity of voices and create better futures together. And we've coached tens of thousands of leaders one-to-one to improve their teams, and, in the process, helped them bring joy back into their work.

We at Altus are a team. In fact, we organized as a team to write this book about teams. We wanted to share our experience working with companies, as well as what we do to make our own team and the teams we partner with amazing. We want you to feel justifiably competent to build a great team—or turn around a lousy one—everywhere you go: in your company, your community, or wherever groups of people try to make things happen together.

In this book, you'll see how specific groups of people have grown into amazing teams. Each chapter shares the story of real people who have struggled and, in many cases, succeeded in growing amazing teams. The names and identifying details have been changed, but the stories are real and reflect our first-hand experience.

You'll see that people often view teams in ways that don't help those teams improve. You'll hear the word "team" for a group of job roles with related tasks, rather than a set of people who jointly hold a promise to create a defined result. We see a lot of wishing, hoping, nudging, demanding, complaining, and shoulder-shrugging (often in that order!), rather than teeing up the conversations that build commitment and coordinate action to accomplish results.

In this book, we build your ability to observe teams, think and act with new perspectives about what's going on, and work within your teams in ways that produce transformative results.

This isn't a recipe book.

There is no recipe for an amazing team. If there was, we'd give it to you. You may have noticed how hard it is to cook a complex dish from a recipe and have it come out amazing without basic cooking techniques, knowledge of how a successful dish should taste and smell, and the patience to let the creation simmer under your attentive eye.

Instead of recipes or rules, we're pointing you toward *yourself* so that *you* can create a better future for your team:

- Bring fresh eyes to see what you've stopped noticing or never knew to observe in the first place.

- Use your heart and gut, as well as your brain, to see what's needed to get team members talking truthfully and usefully.

- Find your ground and take courageous stands for your team to create more value for your organization, customers, and your careers.

We understand that some teams were lousy before you even met them. It's probably not your fault that a team is lousy, but it is your opportunity. We're saying that if you're on a team, leading a team, or responsible for multiple teams, by changing a few things in yourself you can make your teams better.

What kind of changes are we talking about?

First, we want you to **change what you see**. You're already paying attention to some aspects of your team, but are these the most powerful factors? To start, what shared promises do you see? What's the level of each team member's commitment to those promises?

Second, with your attention on the most useful aspects of successful teams, we want you to **see possibilities for improving**. What does "better" look and feel like? To whom would that matter and why? Does it matter to you enough to stay here and stick it out, or do you want to take your attention somewhere else that matters more?

Strengthen your practices—as a person,
as well as a leader and team member—
that enable you to be wise, courageous,
and resourceful.

Third, we want you to **see specific and practical ways to take action** to make your current team better. We want to embolden you to create or join teams that will enable you to make a bigger impact on the world.

Finally, we want you **to strengthen your practices**—as a person, as well as a leader and team member—that enable you to be wise, courageous, and resourceful. We've found these qualities to be contagious—in a very good way. When you show up present, centered, clear on your commitments, and ready to see and address what the team needs, your team members will tend to follow. The few who don't want to be part of an excellent team will go, and that is often for the good.

We've designed this book to help you take these steps.

See this book as a travel guide for your journey of generating amazing teams. You're going to visit teams around the world—teams that may initially seem much better or worse than your own team. Some of these real stories may be within your culture, some outside of it. You'll hear people raise issues you may not have been aware even relate to teams—and then notice that issue is showing up in your own team.

You can start the journey anywhere—wherever you are. Just like there's no proper order in which to visit the countries of South America, there's no set starting point to read this book. Choose a chapter that grabs you and go from there. We take you to visit real teams with real struggles, and we'll help you learn more about your own team as you take this trip. On this journey, you'll see ideas, questions, and practices that stretch the way you think and inspire you to act.

If you're interested in diving deeper, in the next chapter we've summarized the key distinctions—ways of seeing and acting—that underlie our work. You're always welcome to check out the additional resources we've collected online at altusgrowth.com/book. Or contact us if you have questions or want to learn more deeply about building teams.

To make the most of this book, here's what we suggest:

- Take a few moments to **describe what's going on in your team** and what you'd like to be different to achieve better results and increase satisfaction. The worksheet after the *Foundations* chapter and the questions at the end of each chapter can guide your reflection.

- **Stay curious.** How might your insights apply to improving your current team or forming a new one? How can you deepen your understanding of what's happening—and not happening—in your team? What do you take for granted that might keep you from seeing something new? Once you've checked your understanding with others, what next action might you take?

- **Bring this back to yourself** as a team member or leader: What could you develop in yourself to lead these sorts of conversations more effectively? Might you bring more listening, courage, determination, patience, or curiosity? How will you build your ability to show up this way?

- **Be compassionate with yourself and others.** You may find "mistakes" you've made, or that others are making now. Remember, each of you did the best you were able to do. Now, strengthened by the insights from this book, you can achieve more.

- **Invite your team members into a conversation.** What are the next conversations that will help your team become or sustain yourselves as an amazing team—a team that consistently produces results that matter in ways that are healthy and often satisfying to everyone involved?

You're about to embark on a journey to experience with us the promises, pitfalls, and practices of teams around the world. With these fresh insights, go make your team amazing!

Let's get started.

FOUNDATIONS

What It Takes to Make a Team

Kobe Bogaert

We define a Team as ***a specific set of people who commit to a shared promise to create a new future that matters, as declared in the team's mission and goals, and who coordinate their actions to fulfill that promise.***

We choose this definition[7] because the language itself helps you create what you're aiming for in launching the team: a specific future for your company, customers, or community. This future could be anything—easy onboarding for your software's customers (an engineering team), a five-star dinner experience (a restaurant team), or safe bike access (a community team). You form a team because you believe these particular people, working together, are better able to produce that future than you alone or with a group of task-doers who aren't committed to an outcome or coordinating to produce it.

MISTAKING YOUR GROUP FOR A TEAM

One of the first things I notice as I enter companies is that the groups they call teams usually don't meet this definition. Instead, I see groups of people who assume they're on a team because they have

11

similar customers, meet to share information, and report to the same person on the org chart. Frequently these people aim to accomplish individual tasks, rather than a shared outcome. They depend on their leader or project manager to assure some level of coordination across individuals and tasks.

I also notice that the people on these teams-in-name-only are often dissatisfied with what they can accomplish. Though they themselves are working hard, the work doesn't add up to producing something valuable and satisfying for their internal and external customers. They also don't feel great. Rather than being lifted by a sense of camaraderie and tangible support, group members feel isolated—even undermined—as they try to get through the to dos of the day.

For example, a fast-growing healthcare company's executive "team" wasn't producing the operating results needed to stay in business. The executives were working tremendously hard, but performance wasn't improving. Each team member was highly capable yet saw different parts of the situation. They felt so busy that they didn't make time to coordinate the promises and actions of their departments, and their misalignment meant people were unintentionally working against each other.

I also worked with a chief technology officer (CTO) who was an extremely smart software engineer. Though he had a "team" of capable people he respected, he was used to solving problems himself. When team members offered ideas, he was quick to show them why his ideas were better. Over time, they offered fewer and fewer ideas. The CTO became dissatisfied with their lack of proactivity and contributions. As a result, he listened to them even less. Through the course of our work together, he discovered missed business opportunities and incomplete implementations, because his team had come to focus on carrying out his specific directives, rather than accomplishing a shared promise.

Another group was working on highly visible, large construction projects. As their workload ballooned, they weren't making time to coordinate disparate parts of the work, listen and offer help, or think together about how to deal with breakdowns.[8,9,10] They began to miss deadlines and repeat mistakes. According to the CEO, it seemed the "team" frequently lost track of client commitments. Everyone was frustrated, including the CEO. Yet they didn't talk about it.

We want winning teams in sports, and we accept the need to invest in building, nurturing, and growing these teams purposefully so they can achieve success.

WHAT WE CAN LEARN FROM SPORTS TEAMS

Sports was my first experience with teams, as it was for many of us. Growing up in Belgium, my favorite sport was soccer, and to this day I am a big fan. I love teams that are playing together with quick one-touch passes to create space for the final attack. The buildup, the execution, and attention to each other are a joy to watch.

We want winning teams in sports, and we accept the need to invest in building, nurturing, and growing these teams purposefully so they can achieve success. Yet, when we think about our experience with teams in the business world, we very often don't apply the same intentionality or rigor. We lack commitment to shared outcomes and coordinated action, we underinvest in creating and practicing winning plays, and we sidestep genuine, productive conversations. It is these conversations that are the actual drivers of team performance in the workplace.

Over the years, I've worked with executives who firmly believe their teams' problems are simply unsolvable because miscommunication springs from human nature. They believe teams will always be frustratingly misaligned, and they've factored that dysfunction into their approach to managing and into their explanations to company leaders. They are so resigned to dysfunction that they no longer pay attention to what's working in teams and the interactions that produce more of what works.

My experience shows teams can indeed learn and improve, achieving both higher performance and a more satisfying experience for team members. In this chapter, we share ten essential elements that create high-performing teams in sports and in business:

TABLE Ten essential elements of teams

	SPORTS TEAM	QUESTIONS FOR BUSINESS TEAMS
Shared Care (Purpose)	• Be the best. • Leave a legacy.	• What future matters enough. to us that we are choosing to create or join this team?
Shared Promise (Mission)	• Win the championship.	• What does winning look like? • What outcomes do we intend to produce and by when?
Commitment and Alignment	• I want us to win, and I'm giving all I have. • We're working toward the same goal.	• How committed are we to accomplish this? • What does alignment look like? • How will we stay aligned?

Values	• Excellence. • Fair play. • Team first.	• What's important about how we work together that will help us achieve success? • What specific behaviors will demonstrate we're operating from these values?
Standards	• Be at every practice. • Study tapes of previous games. • Be in good condition.	• What standards will help us work together effectively? • What tools and practices do team members need to operate to that standard?
Roles, Planning, and Cooperation	• Each player has a position to play. • Plays are prepared, practiced, and called. • Each player does their best to give others what they need to fulfill their roles.	• What roles do team members play? • What plans do we need to prepare and execute? • How do we need to coordinate plans with other teams? • What skills do we each need to develop to grow collectively into a high-performing team? • What will success look like, and how do we each contribute to that success?
Trust, Inclusion, and Relationships	• Notice each of my teammates' capabilities, intentions, preparation, and determination to win. • Trust the coach. • Support, inspire, and celebrate my team members.	• What are we doing to build trust in the team? • How do we repair mistrust? • How are we welcoming and listening to the voice of each team member? • How are we inviting and including diverse viewpoints? • What are we doing to develop and sustain healthy work relationships between team members?

Mood	• Ambition (versus resignation on losing/deflated teams). • Learning (versus arrogance).	• What are the persistent emotional patterns on this team? How might these reflect the beliefs members hold about our future? • What is more or less likely to happen because our team operates out of these emotions or moods? • How able are we to shift genuinely toward moods that support achieving the future we want?
Accountability and Coordination of Action	• Players are clear on what they need to do: positions, plays, practices. • When we need to change our style of play, we coordinate to make that happen.	• What specific promises are we each making? • What practices and tools do we need to stay coordinated and achieve our promises? • How are we evaluating and improving? • How do we get back on track when promises weren't made, weren't managed, or weren't fulfilled?
Responsibility	• I do everything I can to help the team win. • I will close the gap if a teammate stumbles.	• What else can I do to help the team accomplish our promise? • How are we making sure we each stand for each other's success and that everyone else stands for ours? • Are we willing to ask for and offer help?

I am excited to share with you something remarkable, something hidden right in plain sight:

Each of these ten elements that build a team is created from and sustained by *conversations*.[11]

Pause for a minute and allow this to soak in. Your team is, or is not, on track to achieve a promise because of conversations. Your team works in moods of ambition or resignation because of the conversations you've had or haven't had. Your team coordinates effectively because of conversations, whether in previous meetings, emails, Slack, calendars, or messaging, or conversations in your heads.

For many, this is a crucial shift in understanding. The most fundamental action of team leaders and members is to choose which conversations to have and how and when to have them. As Chalmers Brothers says in *Language and the Pursuit of Leadership Excellence*: Leaders get paid to have effective conversations—that is, conversations that produce specific results that matter to customers and other stakeholders.[12] Regardless of title, all team members contribute to the performance of their team by engaging—skillfully, unskillfully, or not at all—in the conversations that produce the ten elements above.

Why are conversations the key to team results? As we have come to see it, language does more than describe things or to share information.[13,14,15] Crucially, language shapes the world we perceive and what we do with it. It's this generative capacity of language that team leaders and members use when they engage purposefully in important workplace conversations.

I've seen that when a team isn't achieving great results, at least one of these elements is missing or being discussed ineffectively. The key skill of any team leader is to notice which conversations are needed and tee those up in useful ways. Through conversations, team members deepen their commitment to action or suggest other ways of working. They figure out how to navigate through changing business conditions, and they help each other learn and grow.

Let's look more closely at each of the ten elements of teams in organizations and sports.

SHARED CARE (PURPOSE)

A sports team's purpose is to win consistently—even raise the level of play in their sport and become a legendary franchise. Each of the individual team members, coaches, and managers must care deeply about this. If any player doesn't buy into and support this core purpose, team performance will suffer. When a player is in it "just for the money" without passion for the game, commitment to the team, and intent to win, everyone feels it.

Many companies have lofty, carefully worded purpose statements. Yet, when we ask people about what the statement means to them and how this purpose guides their day-to-day operations, we usually find a disconnect. When people don't feel connected to their company's purpose, they default to, "I'm here for the paycheck." This means they're more susceptible to becoming disengaged or leaving for a slightly better offer, making it harder for the company to build effective teams over time. Even more damaging, people who aren't connected to the purpose are less likely to see fresh opportunities that help fulfill that purpose.

Designer Eileen Fisher, whose company is dedicated to "creating products we love, in service of women and the planet,"[16] has engaged team members to explore deep into their supply chain, renew used garments, and design for broader ages. These conversations drive performance and help the company attract the most innovative talent. Purpose points to the most important things we care about and what we are committed to being, doing, or having in the world. When team members connect to a shared purpose, research shows they participate much more powerfully, enthusiastically, and effectively.[17]

CARE

Why Care Is Critical to Teams
Bob Dunham

We care because, as humans, we can imagine some futures we want and some we don't want. Care is our internal emotional compass that orients our attention and action towards specific outcomes and away from others.

When we are clear on what we care about, we choose actions that move us in our preferred direction. Our actions then "take care" of what matters to us. Acting consistently with our care we experience more energy, creativity, and joy. This helps us persist in the face of difficult, confusing, or changing circumstances.

Care matters on teams for three powerful reasons.

First, we always show up with our own cares: building an exciting career, feeding our families, achieving mastery, having fun with co-workers, designing something beautiful, etc. When we're unaware of our cares or see the team's work as irrelevant to what we want, we may drift into "going through the motions," "being busy," or "gaming the system," and this negatively impacts the team. When we see that the team's work—the process and/or the result—takes care of our cares, we bring more energy and determination.

Second, when we create a team culture where our colleagues listen to what we authentically care about, we feel and are seen, respected, and included. This increases our team's connection and resilience, with all the benefits that brings.

Third, the power of shared care in a team makes it possible to create bigger offers that translate into greater impact. The diversity of individual cares on our team helps us craft more robust and valuable possibilities. Then, as we make time to sync up our cares into a shared team care, we have a compass to guide us as a team toward a future we want.[18,19]

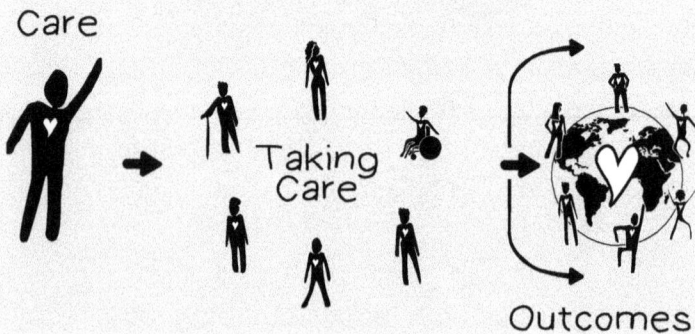

YOU TAKE ACTION TO PRODUCE OUTCOMES YOU CARE ABOUT

Care

Taking Care

Outcomes

SHARED PROMISE (MISSION)

Sports teams usually have a clear mission lasting one or several seasons: "We're aiming to become division champions!"

Successful teams share a mission that captures the outcomes they want to produce and how they will measure success. Goals are easy to define and measure in soccer, but often remain undefined or unshared in organizations. Different interpretations of what success looks like lead to uncoordinated action, which dampens results.

A team is only a team for as long as
it has a shared promise.

A shared promise was one of the elements missing in the healthcare company mentioned earlier. As I asked each executive about the future they were working so hard to create, they began to see each had different definitions of that future and the strategies needed to get there. Once this became clear, they invested time as a team to compare views of the future and define the shared promise they intended to fulfill. This alignment reduced wasted energy and frustration and gave their people sufficient direction to operate as a team, instead of as disconnected groups. The leaders were then able to shift their focus from firefighting to developing effective strategies for continued growth.

No promise, no team. This insight is so important that we've devoted two chapters to the crucial role of shared promises in creating teams. A team is only a team for as long as it has a shared promise. The moment you fulfill (or abandon) your goals, you effectively stop being a team—until you commit to the next shared promise.

COMMITMENT AND ALIGNMENT

Successful sports teams are aligned around the game plan that best fits their talent and competitive environment. For example, will this soccer team be more successful by playing fast and aggressively, or by slowing the game down and playing defensively? Team commitment and alignment are essential to executing any game plan.

Team members who act out of high levels of commitment will do anything that's possible and prudent to accomplish the promise of the team.

The construction company that was missing deadlines had recently promoted two individuals to the executive team. This was their first experience as executives, and they began to see that the commitment required was different than what it was when they managed their respective departments. Newly promoted executives often need thoughtful conversations to understand fully what it means to hold commitment for the entire organization and to learn the actions to do so. Disappointed clients finally prompted the CEO to orchestrate the conversations needed to align the team.

Teams often struggle to assess the commitment of various individual team members. Team members who act out of high levels of commitment will do anything that's possible and prudent to accomplish the promise of the team. This dramatically improves the odds of successfully navigating the inevitable obstacles and breakdowns that are part of every team's experience. When needed, members will "take one for the team"—sacrifice something, such as an opportunity for an exciting project or personal glory, so that the team can be more successful.

Successful teams align on three levels: team members' individual cares (ME), their coordination with each other (WE), and the results they are committed to producing (WORLD).

ME—WE—WORLD

Where You Pay Attention
Bob Dunham

To produce specific results in our companies and communities, we observe, choose, and learn in three dimensions:

The **ME space** is where we each identify what matters profoundly to us. Here, we observe our commitments, moods, emotions, and actions. We listen to our private conversations that shape our internal states, we acknowledge our history, and we pay attention to our body, posture, and well-being. We curate this space as our primary leverage point for seeing possibilities and taking productive action.

The **WE space** is where we connect and coordinate with others. This is the domain of teams, where we have relationships and conversations that can generate commitment and collaboration. We each bring our cares, strengths, and learning edges from our ME space. On healthy teams, these are recognized and developed more deeply than would be possible on our own. Together, we create shared backgrounds, trusting relationships, and future possibilities. In teams, we make requests, promises, and agreements for standards of behavior and performance, so we can take the actions that generate culture and results.

The **WORLD space** is where we choose to make a difference. Here, we observe what matters to people beyond our team, and here we produce outcomes from our commitments and actions. This is also where we experience the consequences of our ME and WE interpretations, declarations, choices, actions, and coordination. We bring what we see and learn about the world back to our team, so together we can make relevant offers and deliver on them.

Leading and participating effectively in teams requires us to observe, design, and take action continually and congruently in all three spaces.[20]

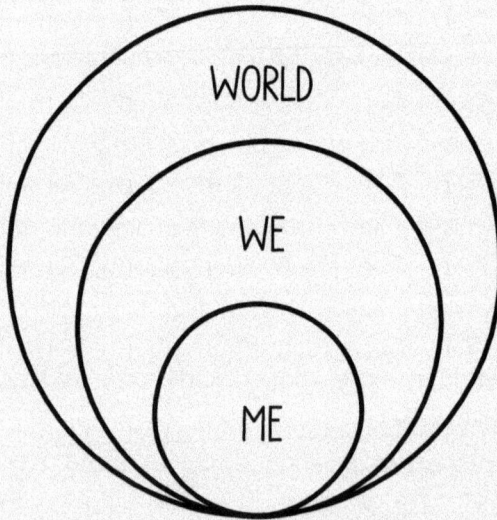

VALUES

Every professional sports team has values that guide how they be-have and relate to each other, how they come together on the field, how they prepare, how they compete, and how they treat each other within the organization and their communities. We've all seen ex-amples of athletes who are very active in communities, living the same values off the field. We've also seen teams slump because a key player was not playing or living by the team values.

When I ask new clients to tell me about their values—without look-ing at their website or the placard on the wall—only a small percent-age can name them, much less describe them. When team members don't share values, or don't know what specific behavior is required to demonstrate those values, we see two predictable outcomes: co-ordination deteriorates and conflict increases. When teams align on a set of shared values and consider regularly how these values guide their work, teamwork and performance improve.

We invited the owners and executives of the construction compa-ny to define their organizational values. We had them identify the specific behaviors for each value that would constitute living or em-bodying the value. It took this particular team about six months to lead in line with their values, at which point each member was able to convene similar conversations with their respective teams. Each team throughout the organization now meets monthly to assess themselves and each other related to these values. These sessions reveal missing conversations that could bring more serious break-downs and performance problems, if not addressed.

STANDARDS

It's obvious that sports teams have standards for practice, partici-pation, dress code/uniform, and behaviors on and off the field. We all accept that a sports team can't be successful without a set of ground rules or rules of engagement, related to ways of acting and interacting. Sports teams also ensure that players are competent and supported to perform to standard. They provide training, coaching, playbooks, equipment, and practice schedules.

Effective teams declare shared standards.

When we look at teams in organizations, standards for performance, practice, and behaviors are often missing or ignored. This happens when leadership avoids the conversations to set standards, develop people to achieve them, and ensure accountability. When I raise this with clients, they respond that they "expected" everyone to know X or that others "should" know Y—even without talking about it.

We each have standards for behavior and performance, and we can inaccurately assume that others share our standards. I hear in fast-growth companies, "We're moving too fast for process and rules." Yet, in each case, the lack of sufficient, specific, shared standards leads to unnecessary misunderstandings, blame, resignations, and poor team performance.

Effective teams declare shared standards around issues involving reliability, quality, timeliness, accountability, customer service, conflict resolution, and types of customer and team member interactions, to name a few. Examples of team standards include always starting meetings on time, requiring all participants to come prepared, defining a set timeframe for follow-up with customers, being clear on who can make what decisions, requiring that members inform the team leader the moment something unplanned occurs, and suggesting that those needing help and guidance always ask for it.

ROLES, PLANNING, AND COOPERATION

Players on a sports team have positions to play and specific tasks required of them. They must fulfill their role for the team to succeed. However, doing individual tasks well is not sufficient for success. Each player must also understand the plan and notice when others aren't where they're expected to be. Players must be prepared to step in to assist or fulfill other roles in real time, adapting plays as situations unfold. Coaches regularly assess player skills in performing scripted and emergent plays, and they encourage good communication during and outside of games to support adaptive collaboration.

In business teams, we also have roles to play and specific tasks to accomplish. Sometimes those are well defined; in other cases, they're not. Without productive conversations to lay out the playbook, clarify roles and interdependencies, and determine how we will communicate and coordinate across roles, we see confusion, frustration, and poor results. Roles, strategies, and priorities often shift in today's dynamic environment—making these conversations even more critical to team success.

TRUST, INCLUSION, AND RELATIONSHIP

We most clearly see the power of relationships in a sports team when it's going through a rough patch. Good teams pull together, support each other, and focus on making the improvements needed. We all know stories about championship teams that were composed of players that—based on any number of metrics—were not the most individually talented in the league. These teams succeeded because players came to trust their teammates to practice even harder, share the ball, and never give up.

I refer to trust and relationships as the "WD-40 of the team." When there's low trust, teams suffer, as members doubt they can depend on one another—which severely limits the types of game plans available. Trust (or more accurately, *distrust*) is often considered undiscussable in organizational settings. For many, trust is a fuzzy concept. As we work with teams, we look at specific aspects of trust—intentions, competence, reliability, listening, etc.—which makes trust something we can discuss and thereby build and rebuild.

Teams committed to inclusion notice which voices are missing or unheard, and they purposefully invite and include *all* voices. Teams gain adaptability from the diverse experiences and unique ways of thinking that each member brings to the table. When a team builds a space safe enough to inquire and talk honestly about team commitment, alignment, and coordination, the team can pull together more strongly and improve. Members feel safe enough to experiment, learn from breakdowns, ask for help, and try again. We know from Project Aristotle[21] and other research[22] that psychological safety is a key enabler of team performance. See the chapters in Section II and III for more on building trust, inclusion, and stronger relationships.

Our moods are the persistent patterns of thinking and emotions that reflect our beliefs about the future.

MOOD

We talk about the moods of athletes regularly: Teams are "on fire" or "in a slump." Championship teams stoke moods of ambition, determination, and solidarity. These carry the team through setbacks and enable teams to persevere until challenges are overcome. Moods are visible in players' posture and movements, in their language, and in the emotions they radiate. Moods are also contagious, which is why managers worry that one discontented player will impact team mood.

Humans are always in a mood—no exceptions.[23] Right now, as you read this sentence, *you* are in a mood. You might be reading from a mood of curiosity—*What will I gain from this book?* Or a mood of ambition—*How can I use what I learn here to make a positive impact on my team?* Or a mood of resignation—*I won't be able to manage these types of conversations.* Our moods are the persistent patterns of thinking and emotions that reflect our beliefs about the future. Once a mood takes hold, it shapes what we notice and actions we take. In this way, our moods can become a self-fulfilling prophecy. With focus and skill, we can cultivate moods that help us reach our goals.

A growing number of successful companies understand the impact of emotional intelligence and agility on their bottom lines. Moods matter on teams, because these persistent emotional tones condition the degree to which members will think creatively, persevere, learn, and cooperate. Workplace moods also directly impact the public identity the organization produces, whether team members want to stay or go, and even individual health and absenteeism. By talking about moods openly, safely, and authentically, team members can notice and challenge their beliefs about the future, make new requests of each other and their organization, and take new action to improve collaboration, coordination, and bottom-line results.

ACCOUNTABILITY AND COORDINATION OF ACTION

No sports team can win if players don't play their positions and run the plays they've practiced. This calls for conversations in which accountability for making plays is defined, discussed, and agreed to ahead of time. In most sports, players must do more than their own prepared task—they must also dynamically coordinate their actions in response to opposing teams. Teams train constantly so players learn to communicate effectively (often without words) under pressure.

Accountability lives in the promises we make to others. Accountability starts with a promise to do something and is completed when it's done.

Terms of Accountability
- You can be accountable only if you make a promise.
- Accountability means fulfilling your promise. If circumstances occur in which this isn't possible, you must manage this in coordination with your team or customer.
- You can never assign accountability. You can hold yourself accountable, and you can request others be accountable to their promises.

Misunderstanding the terms of accountability is a frequent source of team breakdowns, as with the software company mentioned earlier. The CTO would tell people what to do, but he didn't make time to hear whether his team members had fully understood, agreed, or actually committed to doing it. Team members made no promises to do anything, yet dutifully implemented most of what they *assumed* the CTO wanted, with predictably unsatisfactory results. As the CTO began to share the business objectives, make specific requests, and elicit clear promises, results improved. Once team members understood the business context, they became able to make their own promises, coordinate with each other, and hold themselves accountable.

At their core, all workplace teams and organizations may be understood as "networks of commitments," where people make and manage commitments with each other.[24] A high-performing team builds the discipline to create clarity around requesting, making, managing, fulfilling, and accepting delivery of these promises. The more clearly we see the interdependent networks of commitments by which we coordinate action, and the more attention we pay to accountability, the better the team will perform.

AN ORGANIZATION IS A
NETWORK OF COMMITMENTS

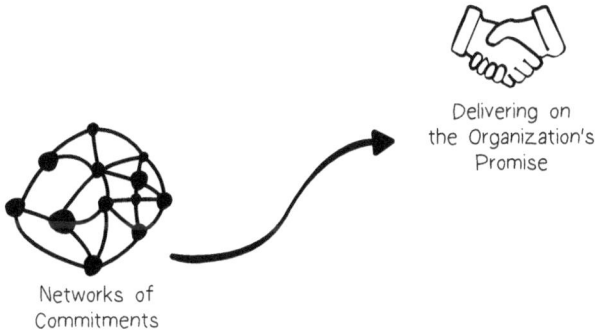

Delivering on
the Organization's
Promise

Networks of
Commitments

RESPONSIBILITY

A team member is **accountable** when they do their individual tasks as they promised. A team member is **responsible** when they keep their eyes on the team's promise and proactively support the team in achieving it. See the *Responsibility Makes the Team* chapter to learn more; we also recommend *The Power of Owning Up* by Bob Dunham and Sameer Dua.[25]

In team sports, members of top teams are constantly looking out for collective success. They push their teammates to improve, they read the field, and they don't let their egos get in the way of winning plays. Championship franchises also know that everyone matters to winning—not only the players on the field, but those on the bench, the coach, the support staff, the back office, and the owner, too.

We see this commitment to responsibility in successful companies, too. We see responsible team members willing to prompt others to do their jobs, and even to assist in doing that work—if that's what it takes for the team to achieve its goals. We see them open conversations about changes in customer needs. We see them call out what's missing or not working well and give the team the opportunity to explore whether they see the same things and what to do about that.

These proactive moves help reveal blind spots sooner rather than later and identify areas where new strategies and competencies may be needed. Responsible team members look beyond their own tasks to take care of their team, coordinate well across interdependencies, and make the most of opportunities to accomplish the team's promise. These team members take a stand of, "I can and will act for the sake of the team's success."

When work groups are frustrated, resigned, or underperforming, we often find these three orientations toward responsibility:

- *We aren't responsible, someone else is responsible.* Responsibility lies elsewhere, outside of ourselves. We're just here to do the job, whether we think it makes sense or not. We are doing what we are being told, and there isn't anything we can do about it. Responsibility lies outside of this team—often, it's the executive team, the board, the customer, or another department.

- *The person who is asking us to do this job is responsible.* We as team members are merely performing what is being asked of us by our leader. Whether our team succeeds, depends on whether our leader sees enough, knows enough, and is smart enough to tell us the right things to do.

- *We are all responsible, but we don't act.* Most of us see what needs to be done, but we're not talking about it. We're hoping someone else will address it.

In my experience, groups of people that have yet to embrace responsibility—or any of the elements above—can step up together and become high-performing teams. The key is changing their conversations.

Team competence is always built from—and sustained by—good conversation. These ten elements provide the rock-solid foundation of successful teams. Conversation is the fastener that binds these elements together.

If you have a group and you want to build a team, start having these conversations:

- For what purpose are we here?
- What do we intend to accomplish?
- How committed are we?
- What values guide us?
- What standards do we need?
- How shall we coordinate across roles?
- How are we strengthening relationships?
- How are we cultivating moods that favor success?
- How are we holding ourselves accountable?
- How are all of us holding responsibility for our promise?

Teams that align on these elements—and commit to ongoing learning and competency-building within them—produce exceptional results, as well as tremendous satisfaction for members. Build your capability to open and sustain these conversations, and you become able to build high-performing teams.

In this book, you'll peek inside team conversations in dozens of organizations around the world. Through examples and practical suggestions, you'll discover what it takes to turn your groups into teams and to make those teams successful.

WORKSHEET

Think of a team that matters to you. This could be you and your peers at work, a team that reports to you, or a team in which you participate in your community.

- How do each of these elements show up on your team right now?

- Where are misunderstandings, differing perspectives, and missing conversations?

- What's missing to make your team amazing?

- What actions might you take to move your team forward?

TEN ESSENTIAL ELEMENTS OF TEAMS	QUESTIONS TO CONSIDER	YOUR NOTES ABOUT YOUR TEAM
Shared Care (Purpose)	• What future matters enough to us that we are choosing to create or join this team?	
Shared Promise (Mission)	• What does winning look like? • What outcomes do we intend to produce and by when?	
Commitment and Alignment	• How committed are we to accomplish this? • What does alignment look like? • How will we stay aligned?	

Values	• What's important about how we work together that will help us achieve success? • What specific behaviors will demonstrate we're operating from these values?	
Standards	• What standards will help us work together effectively? • What tools and practices do team members need to operate to that standard?	
Roles, Planning, and Cooperation	• What roles do team members play? • What plans do we need to prepare and execute? • How do we need to coordinate plans with other teams? • What skills do we each need to develop to grow collectively into a high-performing team? • What will success look like, and how do we each contribute to that success?	
Trust, Inclusion, and Relationships	• What are we doing to build trust in the team? • How do we repair mistrust? • How are we welcoming and listening to the voice of each team member? • How are we inviting and including diverse viewpoints? • What are we doing to develop and sustain healthy work relationships between team members?	

Mood	• What are the persistent emotional patterns on this team? How might these reflect the beliefs members hold about our future? • What is more or less likely to happen because our team operates out of these emotions or moods? • How able are we to shift genuinely toward moods that support achieving the future we want?	
Accountability and Coordination of Action	• What specific promises are we each making? • What practices and tools do we need to stay coordinated and achieve our promises? • How are we evaluating and improving? • How do we get back on track when promises weren't made, weren't managed, or weren't fulfilled?	
Responsibility	• What else can I do to help the team accomplish our promise? • How are we making sure we each stand for each other's success and that everyone else stands for ours? • Are we willing to ask for and offer help?	

SECTION ONE

WHY TEAMS?

WHY MAKE A TEAM?

How Teams Deliver
When Groups Cannot

Pam Fox Rollin and Kobe Bogaert

- Why do groups of high performers often fail to perform well together?

- What can you do when you have a group, and you need a team?

- What benefits arise for the business and for your career when you turn groups into teams?

Janine clicked through the initiative dashboards. Given the delay, she knew something was off, but what? Had they set unrealistic deadlines? Were they short of people? Short of budget? Had they hit a technology roadblock that no one was willing to communicate?

As the just-hired vice president of infrastructure optimization for a global retail giant, Janine was tasked with putting this initiative back on course, and she was determined to do so. This wasn't just any initiative. This program will spend about half a billion dollars over several years to re-platform company technology, shift more to the cloud, boost security, and strengthen optimization, which itself could recoup the entire investment over the next decade.

Janine inherited a cross-functional "team" of thirteen people: five senior directors loaned from each of the five business divisions, four technology experts, two finance reps, a purchasing leader, and a project management specialist. When the leader who assembled this group left six months ago, the group made a case that they already had a plan and just needed to execute it, which did not require a leader. Since each of the members as individuals were rated as excellent or top performers, the C-suite decided to let them do just that.

But things were not going well. Over the past month, the two business unit heads most dependent on new technology began questioning the CTO about execution delays. The CTO decided to ask the new VP, Janine, to focus full-time on the initiative and figure out how to get it on track.

SEEING WHAT WAS MISSING: A TEAM

How could a group of top performers get so far behind on a high-visibility initiative? Janine brought us in to tee up conversations necessary to pinpoint and address the cause of the delays. We interviewed the team members and their internal customers.

Here's what we found:

- Each interviewee thought this transformation was "a good idea for the business." However, they each had somewhat different visions of what successful completion would be.

- Members each considered themselves responsible for their own tasks on the project plan. None of them saw themself as personally responsible for collaborating to produce the transformation for the overall business.

In other words, this was *not* a team. This was a group of people who had agreed (or at least not disagreed) to go to meetings and accomplish tasks that might over time enable the company to move in a general direction.

Because there was no **shared commitment to a specific goal**, members were unable to describe what was missing to accomplish the initiative. Because there was no **shared commitment to coordinate**, members were unwilling to risk their own interpersonal and reputational comfort to call out and address siloed information, changing market requirements, missed handoffs, etc. Members showed up to meetings and politely reported on their individual tasks without positively challenging each other to ensure the team created the value that the company needed.

This uncoordinated work created delays in two ways. First, the individual tasks yielded information that needed to inform other people's work: Slow and haphazard communication forced rework or idling while waiting for other work to be done. Second, since the pace of change in the company, market, and technology of course didn't stop for this initiative, each member was learning about, weighing, and adjusting for these changes on their own, which kept them endlessly out of alignment with each other. This fostered endless loops of "Why did they (or didn't they) do that?" "Why wasn't I told?" and "Why bother?"

As a result, it wasn't much fun to work on this initiative. Though group members were polite in their meetings and emails, they knew they weren't accomplishing much and were eager not to end up personally tarnished for what was likely to be a disappointing effort. Members made sure their own pieces of work shined. They verbally offered to "support" each other, but they didn't back this up with action. Additionally, their colleagues not assigned to this initiative resented the budget and attention being spent for little benefit, and there were unaddressed bad feelings between those who were working on the initiative and those who were not.

*What was missing was "teaming"—the
act of transforming a group of people into
an aligned and coordinated force.*

It would be easy to say that what was missing was a leader. In our view, this misses the point. If the group needs a leader to forge the shared commitment and coordination, that's fine. Elevate or bring in a leader, like Janine, who will do this. Yet, we have seen many teams who took it on themselves to clarify the goal and rally their execs into alignment. What was missing was "teaming"—the act of transforming a group of people into an aligned and coordinated force to design, sustain, or change a business program to produce a different result.

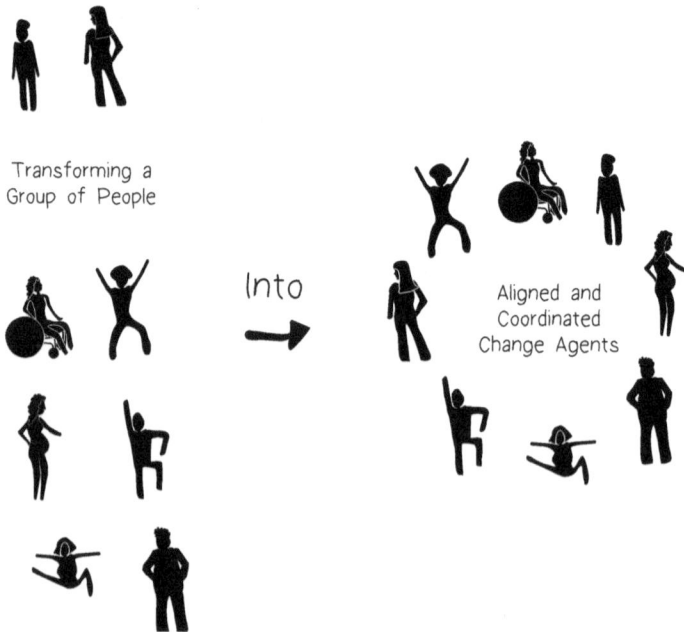

Transforming a
Group of People

Into

Aligned and
Coordinated
Change Agents

WHY DO WE WIND UP WITH GROUPS INSTEAD OF TEAMS?

First, we are used to groups: clusters of people often in the same proximity or function reporting to the same person. They see themselves as doing valuable tasks that help that function or the business, but they don't share a clear and powerful commitment to a defined future and to coordinating to achieve it. Though they may be called a team, really they are a group. The members of groups like this act basically as contractors who happen to be paid as employees.

Second, most organizations evaluate and reward individual performance. When we see companies with thriving teams, they evaluate and reward both team performance and individual results. Typical business cultures and organizational routines set people up to form groups rather than teams. Goal setting and periodic evaluation tend to focus on accomplishing the tasks assigned to the role, rather than contributing whatever is needed for the team to accomplish their outcomes. Leadership development often focuses on individual "high potentials," promotion and succession matrices all but ignore team performance, and decision authority demands "one throat to choke."

Third, many people simply don't know how to be in a team. Having grown up in school systems that reward individual performance, people often lack the competency to identify and have the missing conversations. They suspect (correctly!) that pulling together as a team will require more time talking about what's going on and what should be happening. If they try to have these conversations with little skill, they indeed may experience conflict, hurt feelings, time wasted, blaming and shaming, and other dysfunctions. As Bob Dunham says, "blind spots in teams are cultural—they are not individual failings."[26]

Fourth, team leaders often focus on managing team members, not on generating and delivering on a promise and outcomes as a team. They don't know the conversations teams need—the ten conversations introduced in the previous chapter. Many people have never experienced real teams, beyond participation in sports, so they aren't aware of what is missing. The irony is that their typical complaints about working as a team—lack of commitment, shirking, private agendas, defensiveness—diminish when leaders focus on developing real teams.

SEEING WHAT ELSE WAS MISSING: A COMMITTED "CUSTOMER"

Our initial interviews pinpointed important gaps at the executive level:

- Each internal executive "customer"—the business unit leaders, CTO, and CFO—considered someone else responsible for ensuring the success of the initiative.

- Each executive wanted "their" rep on the team to win—to gain more influence than other group members, to shine brighter and earn promotions, to bring more intel back to their "own" team, to give less and get more.

So, while the executives wanted the initiative to succeed, they were playing a game that didn't make space for forging a team that would drive success. They were playing a form of the classic Prisoner's Dilemma.[27] If everyone cooperates, everyone wins. However, if some quietly withhold cooperation, their "side" may come out ahead. This is not the only executive game we see that makes it unlikely teams will form, but it is one of the most common unless there's a CEO who insists on a different game.

In generative leadership, we identify the role of a Committed Customer as crucial to the success of a team. Who is this customer? It's the person or team who asked for the change who intends to reap substantial value when it is accomplished. Competent, committed customers will therefore keep in touch with the team and help it secure what is needed to succeed. A team's customer can be "above" the team in the organization (as in this case), external to the team (as a major client would be), or, the leader may be acting as a customer for the commitments of their team. An effective team truth-tells to someone who is actually committed to results from their work.

OPENING THE CONVERSATIONS

Janine realized that no amount of clarifying and re-delegating tasks was going to produce success. What she needed to do was form a team backed by executive customers committed to success.

She started with the execs. Janine and the CTO went to each of the executives involved and asked how important it was to them specifically that this group produce results for the company. It was not a "gotcha" question. They sincerely wanted to know how this initiative stacked up against other priorities, and what the executives were and weren't willing to risk to have this initiative succeed. They aimed to get beyond lip service and hear the executives' real concerns about what would happen if the initiative succeeded and what might happen if the initiative failed or only partially succeeded.

It became apparent that the executives expected disappointment, so they angled for their people to look good and grab territory as the initiative fell apart. They had good business reasons for wanting their function to come out of this on their feet, yet preparing for partial failure prevented the group from becoming a team that succeeds.

Through conversations, Janine and the CTO were able to forge genuine commitment to the initiative on the part of the key execs. This is the kind of commitment that only emerges after full conversations about real concerns.

Gaining real commitment requires a deep level of honesty about their own capabilities.

We've seen many leaders give up before gaining full commitment. Instead, they temporarily satisfy themselves with head nods and hope, because gaining real commitment requires a deep level of honesty about their own capabilities and because it takes too much time. Of course, not succeeding ultimately consumes even more time and money. Leaders in companies where teams thrive take the time to gain real commitment to key initiatives and postpone projects where they cannot drive sufficient commitment to succeed.

Once the execs were on board, each could tell "their" team member to cooperate fully. Yet, Janine knew this would not be sufficient. Why? Because even if the members of the team were willing to cooperate fully, they didn't yet have practices to do so, nor did they have a common view of the future they intended to create. They had spent many months working in individual tasks coordinated through silent non-collaboration. They knew how to thrive in that ineffective environment. As has often been said, every system is perfectly organized to get the results it is now getting—and for sure this applies to teams.

Janine engaged the initiative members in forging a common goal and redesigning their practices as a team. With our help, the team rebuilt their definition of success—this time with more specificity. They interviewed and visited internal customers to identify the elements that mattered most, and they committed individually and as a team to producing together a capability that would actually satisfy the needs of those customers. As they became committed to succeeding together, their energy rose, and they became curious how they could help each other do more, faster, and better.

They then asked, "How do we need to partner with each other to be able to produce that successful outcome?" Here, they made many changes. They shifted from organizing around and reporting on tasks to focus on the outcome and reporting on progress in achieving the outcome. They redesigned their meetings from reports of tasks done to designing the next elements together and problem-solving challenges that arose. They scheduled frequent meetings with internal customers and external resources so they could read early signals of changing needs and technologies, share their findings across the team, and design those changes into their solutions. This allowed them to stay aligned as a team in a rapidly moving environment.

How do we need to partner
with each other to produce
that successful outcome?

As a result of these changes—created by fresh conversations with the executives and the team—the initiative team fulfilled its promise to transform the company's technology platform in ways that met the needs of internal customers and made financial sense for the business. Given the high failure rate of similar initiatives across retail and other industries, accomplishing the goal was a huge success that Janine and the executive team made sure to celebrate.

The success of the team also created justified confidence that this company could take on even larger initiatives. The thirteen team members were energized to take the practices that worked here and adapt them to build real teams throughout the company. They and their execs became more skilled in holding conversations that are essential for doing hard things: Are we really committed to the same outcome? Where are we losing trust in each other? How can we repair trust? How could we make better use of each other's skills and resources to accomplish more together?

WHAT BENEFITS COME FROM THE HARD WORK OF MAKING A TEAM?

As Janine's company discovered, real teams produce real benefits:

- **Teams produce bigger results more consistently than groups.**
  In our experience, teams make and fulfill bigger promises than a set of individuals executing tasks. Hands down, every time. Teams don't run on whims—they think things through, so they can truly align. With encouragement, most teams are willing to think bigger, to create the most valuable future they can. Plus, when you know "you're in it" with other people, and they have your back, you give that extra bit of work, insight, or help that adds up to a bigger result.

- **Teams navigate change better than groups.**
  When people have a shared commitment to reach the goal line (even when that line must move or change shape), they deal more effectively with the ambiguity and personal risk of change. People on teams share information and insights faster than in groups. They feel supported to admit they don't know how to do something, so they are more available to learn from people on and beyond the team. Team members speak up about unexpected breakdowns and help each other more consistently than people who don't share a common commitment.

- **Teams develop people more rapidly than groups do.**
  You are more willing to hear useful feedback, we'd bet, from a team member who shares your determination to create a result. Additionally, team members actually want you to get better and will help accordingly because your competence helps the team succeed.

Because of these benefits, leaders—at all levels—who know how to build and sustain teams are in high demand.

WHAT ARE THE BENEFITS TO YOU OF TURNING YOUR GROUP INTO A TEAM?

- **You become someone for whom the best people want to work.**
  With remote and hybrid work, talent markets have become less tethered to geography, so companies everywhere can aim to attract your talent. Increasingly, winning the war to hire and keep your talent depends on culture. Much of culture depends on the quality of teaming. Your best hires will want to know: Do your teams make the most of the talented people on the team? Will I be able to develop within this team? Are people on your teams really committed to a shared outcome, or do they undermine each other? Are your teams knocking it out of the park, and are they rewarded accordingly?

- **You become someone who brings the best people with you.**
  The most effective experienced executives with whom we work seldom struggle to hire. Instead, dozens of stellar people who have worked with them over the course of their careers want in. Often, the decisive factor is knowing this leader will build a team that's up to something big, and that they will be capable of accomplishing it together.

- **With the best people, organized in effective teams, you can take on bigger challenges and succeed.**
  If you want to make a difference, invent new solutions, solve challenging problems, develop capable people, and experience the rewards of a successful career, you'll need teams.

TEAMS ARE A CHOICE

Angélica Del Carpio
EXECUTIVE LEADER, COACH, AND ALTUS CONTRIBUTOR

Do I really want a team?

Maybe I could get results faster and more easily by relying on myself and contracting out specific tasks I don't enjoy or don't do well.

I spent a big part of my career operating this way—in corporate work, as well as consulting. I committed to create results, and I took singular responsibility for making it happen.

This is the game of the solo player—and it's enticing. My work, my solutions, my rewards. No bothering with people in all their pesky humanity. No time wasted developing, encouraging, and involving them.

Most of us have a lot of practice playing the solo game as determined students and outstanding individual contributors.

Promoted for our individual chops, we agreed to take on a team. As one my CEO clients said, "I'll offload as much of the tedious work to these people as possible."

Then he discovered, as I had, that solo leadership scales poorly. Big ambitions tend to require powerful thinking from diverse and committed partners and well-coordinated actions from people who trust each other.

This leaves me—and you—with choices:

- Go as far as your own drive and skills can take you, and be OK with playing small.

- Get a group of task-doers and operate as the hub and driving force, always vigilant for misalignment among group members who lack commitment beyond doing tasks.

- Invest in building a team with shared ambition, then do what it takes to win big together.

If you choose the team option, this book is for you.

SHOULD ALL GROUPS BECOME TEAMS?

In the hundreds of companies with whom we've worked, we've seen only two situations where it's better to manage a group of task-doers than build a team:

- **When you are committed to keeping your agenda private.** Occasionally, people value the secrecy of the business goal so highly—and consider their associates so untrustworthy— that they choose to parse out tasks, rather than create shared commitment to a future. This is sometimes appropriate for a defined period associated with a business transaction, such as a merger.

Beyond this limited circumstance, we find this reasoning overused by leaders who haven't learned how to lead through teams or to navigate varied points of view. Because of the leaders' limitations, their companies become misaligned "groups of groups," stumbling in the dark to produce anything of value.

- **When the talent you need is unwilling or unable to operate as a team.**
  We have run across rare cases of highly capable people who will simply not coordinate productively with others. Usually, the organization will still choose to operate as a team and carve out one or two pieces of the work to be managed separately. This approach has its own costs, but it can work.

  It's not unusual for us to hear, "You will never get these people to operate as a team." What that means is, "I haven't seen it, and the couple of things I've tried haven't worked yet." Take this as a prompt to address the basics below. You may be amazed who decides to join as full members of your team.

RECOMMENDED ACTIONS

- **Determine whether you have a group or a team.** If it's a group, do you need a team?

- **Assess what's in place and what's missing to function as a team.** For example, do you have a clear customer who is committed to the team's success? Or is this just an executive asking for updates and pushing deliverables?

- **Hold open conversations with your colleagues** to find out if they want to build a real team with a shared goal and commitment to coordinate. Note that you can have transformative conversations, whether or not you have the formal leader title.

- **Make sure the future you intend to create is worth your time to build a team.** Find others with complementary capabilities who want to commit to this result and who are eager to work as a team.

FORGING A TEAM AT THE TOP

Pam Fox Rollin

- Does your most senior leadership group meet the standards of a team?

- Would it be worth your hard work to create a real team at the top?

- If so, what are the steps to make that happen?

"We need to start with a big change, something that will wake up the team."

It was early December, and Michael was thinking ahead to the first Monday in January—his first day as CEO of this US-based public company. After several years as a senior vice president, he was the clear choice to replace the retiring CEO; only the swift timing came as a surprise.

"There's no way we'll succeed this year with the exec team the way it is. They're all strong or decent in their roles, and I don't want to get rid of anyone—at least not yet. But there's tons of dysfunction across this company, and this group isn't solving it. Actually, I wonder if some of the problems stem from us," Michael told me.

In support of the CEO transition, I attended executive team meetings, so I knew what he meant. Weekly meetings were polite but dull, often centered on spreadsheets that had everyone looking at their iPads or squinting at screens. One by one, VPs of various functions were ushered into each meeting to share a win or explain a breakdown. Cross-functional problems were raised, discussed for the allotted time on the agenda, and often left unresolved.

---

*We talked about their hopes and fears
as their peer is elevated to CEO, their
concerns, what made them committed to
staying here, and what they're doing to
strengthen the company.*

The overall mood of the executives seemed resigned and politely distrustful, with occasional fireworks that everyone did their best to forget. It reminded me of many (but not all!) of the executive teams with whom I'd worked across industries. To paraphrase Tolstoy, most senior teams are unhappy and dysfunctional in their own ways.[28]

WHAT THE C-TEAM SAW WAS MISSING

Throughout that December, I spent 1:1 time with each executive team member, asking how they saw the business opportunity ahead, and how this team was or was not operating to make good on that opportunity. We talked about their hopes and fears as their peer is elevated to CEO, their concerns, what made them committed to staying here, and what they're doing to strengthen the company. We also discussed what they had chosen not to do that would be useful and why they were holding back. We agreed that each conversation was confidential, yet I would be allowed to share themes with the whole group.

What I heard was sufficient to create that "wake up" moment the new CEO wanted for his first day in January. I cataloged seven changes that each of the eight executives wanted to make in how they worked together. Yet, none of them had made an effective request or offer to initiate these changes. I suspect this was because each of them thought they were alone or there were too few people willing to make a change. As one executive said, "Sometimes on weekends I think about what I might do to improve this team and this company . . . and then I think, 'Screw it, it won't change,' and I go read a book."

Their missing requests included:

- Let's take a clear and joint stand on the next phase of growth for our business.

- Let's figure out what we can expect from each other. I want to hear what everyone thinks about me and my group directly, not through grapevine whisperings.

- Let's stop blaming problems on one group or another. Instead, let's figure out how we solve problems by getting our VPs and directors to work with each other, rather than scrambling to sidestep blame.

- Let's take control of our agendas and commit to discussing what's most important first.

WHAT THEY CHOSE TO DO

On that first Monday, the new CEO gathered the group and spoke simply and powerfully about the opportunities and risks for the business. He said that the people in this room—as a collective, not as individuals—will make the difference between success and failure. Then he had me share the themes I had heard from each of them.

They discovered that they were all dissatisfied with how they operate at the top. And, most important, none of them thought the business will succeed if this executive group continues as a thin layer of co-ordination slapped on top of the silos that actually run the business. The mood in the room shifted immediately from polite resignation to shock. "What, everyone else sees these problems, too?" Amid the shock were moments of possibility, then doubt that they could actually lead differently.

Just as they had become great as individual heads of functions, they can—and will—learn to become great as a genuinely effective senior team.

The CEO was ready for their doubts. He said making changes would be hard for him, too, but just as they had become great as individual heads of functions, they can—and will—learn to become great as a genuinely effective senior team. He shared a new set of "Rules of the Road" and his specific thoughts on what it would take for this effort to succeed.

Then, the CEO asked to hear any issues that might get in the way of a commitment to functioning in this new way. Their biggest concern was the time it would take to operate as a team, and how that would pull them away from their parts of the business—possibly even damaging performance. Michael readily acknowledged they would be spending more time together, as it was critical to spend their time talking directly and usefully about the most important topics. He pointed out that currently much of their time—whether in the full group or not—was spent putting out fires and dealing with escalations that came because the business was not managed cohesively. Their time would be better spent making hard decisions about what they would and would not be doing, and then coaching next-level managers to lead the business forward.

Michael committed to supporting this shift by staying super-focused on this team, leading clearly, cohesively, and effectively; adjusting incentives over time in favor of the good of the business overall; resourcing the team with professional coaching; and committing his time. He asked for the group's commitment to work in this new way, and they gave it.

SO, WHAT HAPPENED?

The CEO kept his word to stay focused on getting executives working as a team. For example, he refused to become the arbiter of disputes, as the former CEO had been. Instead, when disputes emerged, he called in all relevant parties, forged an agreement on criteria for a good solution, then sent them off to go jointly create that solution. After that, he urged them to make a plan for leading it forward, without needing to insert the CEO in the process.

In February, we implemented a simple but powerful quarterly senior team self-assessment that efficiently pinpointed the next areas of focus: ensuring the most important issues surfaced quickly and confirming that cascading communications were in sync throughout the company. That year, the executive team made a bold strategic move that would have been impossible to execute in the old, disjointed way of leading. About half of the team members grew and thrived, and the other half left within 18 months, replaced by new leaders committed to the company's bold future.

In many organizations, it's the executive group that least meets the standards we hold for teams.

The most critical impact occurred outside the executive boardroom. Their next-level reports noticed that the executive team was serious about making long-needed big decisions and dropping the blame culture. They also saw many VPs and directors stepping up to lead initiatives to address the gaps and create new offerings. This simply was not possible until they knew the executive team was aligned on the future of the business and determined to work together to make it so.

WHY MAKE A TEAM AT THE TOP?

In many organizations, it's the executive group that least meets the standards we hold for teams. But does it matter? Is having a team at the top—a group of people who make a shared promise and coordinate to fulfill it—so important to company success that it's worth the hard work to make it happen?

My experience supporting senior teams for more than 20 years says yes. The more the top group of executives meets the definition of a high-performing team, the greater the organization's performance—and satisfaction.

DOES YOUR EXECUTIVE TEAM OPERATE AS A TEAM?

As people watch your top team, what are they learning about being a team?

Are we committed to a shared promise?

Do we help each other succeed?

Do we provide clarity and support to our entire organization?

This claim is also supported by research into what's called "top management teams" (TMTs) in the academic literature.[29] This research is sparse compared to research on board governance, CEO performance, and teams everywhere else in the organization. In a way this isn't surprising—senior executives don't want to be studied, especially at the depth needed for research into the link between their actual behaviors and business outcomes. Published findings validate and reinforce our experience from working with executive teams and confidential conversations with CEOs who have worked with and without real teams at the top.

HOW SENIOR TEAMS POWER OR DAMAGE COMPANY PERFORMANCE

Let's look at the two parts of the definition of a team (as opposed to a group of people who interact and have some common interest).

First, **teams make a shared promise.**[30] They promise to produce a certain type of future for their organization. For top management teams, the promise of the team reflects the entire promise of the company. Here's what investors, customers, employees, regulators, and communities can expect from this entity. The more the entire team shares the promise and commits to creating that sort of future, the more likely they are to achieve it.

What happens when executive group members are not fully invested in the commitment to create a shared future? Here are the breakdowns[31] I repeatedly see across all sizes and structures of companies:

- **Top executives don't have a common picture of what they are aiming to accomplish.** Often, they don't even know that they're not aligned. So, as these leaders work across the organization, they create misunderstanding, waste, gaps in operations and service, and needless conflict, as the middle levels aim to reconcile different directives.

- **Top executives may share a common picture of the intended future, but they aren't highly committed to creating that future.** They're committed to something else, such as making a name for themselves (for example, becoming known as the CTO who created the best AI implementation in this industry), maximizing their compensation (often linked to share price and individual targets, rather than fulfilling the overall promise of the company), or making sure that if a big error occurs, it doesn't come from their group. This sends mixed messages across the company, resulting in more confusion, slow performance, and waste.

Given the breakdowns produced when senior executives don't share a genuine commitment to producing a common future, how can this even happen? Why is it that some CEOs and senior team members don't demand clarity and full commitment from their colleagues?

Here's what I've heard from executives, along with issues reflected in their comments:

- "We'll never get everyone on the same page."
  Resignation, inexperience with effective teams

- "Executives will always be working their own angle."
  "We can't afford to lose Brian as CTO, though, yes, he's always working his own game."
  Politics over a shared commitment

- "We're too busy to put in the time it would take to get on the same page."
  Overwhelm, ineffective prioritization

- "As CEO, it really falls to me to make the decisions. I need strong performers, not a team."
  Conflation of decision-making authority and team standards

These frequent comments reveal the importance of underlying—and often unspoken—assumptions about leadership performance and rewards. Working with hundreds of senior teams have shown us that it's essential to bring these beliefs into the light with respect and thoughtfulness, while helping team members examine each belief and possibly forge new ones to create their overall game together.

FORGE A TEAM AT THE TOP

Susan Molineaux
SERIAL BIOTECH CEO AND BOARD MEMBER

Your top team makes or breaks the company. Not only do leaders need to be top-of-their-game in their area of expertise, they must also work well together as a coordinated team. Bringing this about takes considerable attention and input from me as CEO, but the effort is well worth it.

Without alignment at the top, rifts and dysfunction spread through the company. This creates wasted work, missed opportunities, and the sort of quiet dissatisfaction that causes your best people to accept other offers. Biopharma is a talent-constrained industry. Losing good people because of misaligned leadership is expensive and delays bringing therapies to market.

What Pam talks about here—forging common commitment and improving coordination—is essential to creating a top team that works.

As CEO, I have to be committed to building a team that thinks better together than any of us can alone. This doesn't mean we rely on consensus decisions. Instead, each team member knows their perspective will be valued so they speak up without hesitation, which allows us to run on data and insights, rather than individual agendas. Another benefit of investing time and resources in building an open-minded, high-trust senior team is that each functional leader learns to lead this way. This doesn't happen by itself, which is why I work with consultants like Pam and Heather.

A final thought: Don't mistake style for substance. The best teams I've created include people of all disciplines, experiences, and personalities. What we have in common is that we're all pointed at the same goal and committed to helping each other get there.

Now let's look at the second criteria of a team: **that they coordinate effectively to create the future.**[32]

What happens when members of the executive group do not maintain coordination as the organization takes action? Here are the most common breakdowns:

- **Something goes wrong, and the blame game fires up.** As you've no doubt experienced, breakdowns happen all the time. No plan is ever implemented as originally conceived. Product design gets bogged down in competing user requests. The supply chain falters. Engineers find a fatal flaw or a better way. Salespeople keep promoting the old stuff. Customers find your new thing incompatible with their old things, etc.

  In the absence of clear and supportive (meaning constructive, not "nicey-nice") top team conversations, people across the organization tend to over- or under-escalate breakdowns, aim to pin the problems on someone else, misalign funding with investment needs, and slow down implementation.

- **"Fatal drift" occurs, and the senior group doesn't address it.** Drift happens when people critical to projects are pulled away to other initiatives—usually because the executive team moves on to the next bright shiny goal without revoking or resourcing the last one. We also see drift when senior teams don't keep track of commitments and hold themselves accountable for achieving the results intended. Drift happens because senior team members act as customers accountable only for their own functional initiatives, not for the organization's overall commitments.

- **The overall implementation plan doesn't work and needs to be revised.** The most frequent cause of this breakdown is insufficient deliberation and negotiation as the project was chartered and launched. Senior executives who are skillful in many aspects of leadership fail to meet their own standards when they sit with the executive team.

Given the value of coordination at a senior level, how does this neglect happen? Why do some senior groups fail to maintain effective communication about major initiatives?

Here's what executives have told me:

- *"Our VPs and directors can handle implementation. We've got more important things to do."*
  This is true as long as the senior team maintains its role as customers accountable for the overall promises of the organization and their coordination with each other. Committed customers stay engaged.

- *"Let's be real . . . we didn't hire SVPs who care about collaboration. The board just wanted rockstars in all the seats."*[33]
  Never hire for functional skills and expect to get constructive team behavior for free.

- *"If I ask about our other executives' initiatives, they'll start mucking about in mine. Better to just keep my nose to myself."* Self-protection is the norm for leaders who lack experience with effective senior teams.

When senior leaders are uniformly committed, you can feel the energy throughout the company.

Forging a real team at the top addresses each of these breakdowns. When senior leaders are uniformly committed to creating a shared future and staying in valuable conversations to achieve it, you can feel the energy throughout the company. Yes, it takes work, but it's worth it. And, as a CEO or senior team member, you are there to make it happen.

RECOMMENDED ACTIONS

- **Make sure the CEO fully understands the value of the change and is committed to making it happen.** Many CEOs find they need to become fiercely persistent in holding useful conversations, being more influenced by other points of view, and actively coaching their execs (and turning their execs into leader-coaches).

- **Bring in a coach to support the CEO and team.** While a thoughtful CEO can lead the effort, she cannot simultaneously design and drive the process, accurately register the impact of her behaviors on others, and thoroughly coach herself and others through the process. Experienced executive team coaches observe and listen thoughtfully, bring clarifying insights to team breakdowns, build the next level of leadership mindsets and skillsets, and co-design practices the team can sustain.

- **Have a shared future worth the investment.** Engage the senior team and many others throughout the organization in a rhythm of strategic conversations to design the future. The real plan is not what's on the Gantt chart. It's what's in the heads of every decision maker in your organization, including the front lines.

- **Put in the time.** The senior team requires at least a day together each month, plus as-needed huddles and workgroups. Most top teams have 90-minute meetings each week; typically, these focus on operating issues they should be empowering others to handle. Top teams do best when they give themselves generous work sessions to consider the biggest strategic opportunities, take stands together on the thorniest cross-unit and cross-functional challenges, and become highly skilled in team communication (such as working through conflict, facing and addressing hard feedback, asking for commitment) so they can bring these skills to the whole organization.

- **Be persistent, honest, and supportive.** It's natural that people backslide to what feels comfortable—which is what they've done before. This process needs you, as the CEO or change agent, to speak the truth without blame: "We said we'd do X, and I see we're still doing Y. Do we still believe this shift is worth making, and if so, what will we do differently, starting now?"

- **Implement a dashboard to keep you on track.** Make or ask your coach for a simple, highly relevant team assessment to complete each quarter. Identify and commit to the few top actions for the team to lead more effectively together in the quarter ahead.

MID-LEVEL TEAMS DRIVE CHANGE

Maribell González

- Can organizational change succeed if senior leaders aren't on board from the start?

- What does it take to launch and achieve successful change?

- How do you build a team to lead the change across a company?

A 75-year-old government-owned bank was struggling. With more than 10,000 employees and millions of customers, the bank was essential to this Caribbean country's economy. The bank had long been considered a political arm of the country's president, and there had never been a president with banking experience.

In 2014, a new president arrived who did have industry experience. According to his evaluation, the bank was twenty years behind in the technology and processes required to compete effectively in its market sector. He chose to bring in external banking leaders to modernize the organization.

Bringing people from outside, especially the senior management team, was interpreted by long-time employees as a slap in the face.

They felt their work was not appreciated. Immediately, a rift opened between the old and new people, who came in committed to modernizing the institution at all costs.

My team and I were invited to design and deliver training for the organization's leaders. An internal employee satisfaction survey conducted by the bank showed that 65% of employees believed that leadership, innovation, commitment, and the right attitudes needed for organizational success were missing. We then interviewed employees and leaders, including the director of training, who had been with the bank for sixteen years. She described how the new president's vision was quite different from the vision of previous leaders. Soon, we realized that the bank required more than leadership training.

The institution needed a cultural change that would generate the leadership required to heal the differences among new and longtime employees, align their work, and accomplish the modernization.

The team defined an ambitious promise: to build a culture of leadership and commitment that goes beyond individual people.

DEFINING THE PROJECT AS A PROMISE

From these conversations, the director of training was able to build a sponsor team including the vice president of human resources, director of development, vice president of strategic planning, human resource internal consulting lead, and a regional sales manager. The team defined an ambitious promise: to build a culture of leadership and commitment that goes beyond individual people—a culture that reflected and guided those who worked in the organization.

We projected that a culture change of this magnitude would take at least three years, and, as customary, would start with the commitment of executive management. Successful culture change needs the support and aligned behavior of senior leadership to be successful across a company. The first phase would focus on engaging the president and his team of vice presidents (24 people). Once this was under way, we would start a second phase engaging the general directors and regional sales directors (120 people).

We announced that participation in the process would be voluntary. Those who chose to participate would do so out of inspiration and conviction, not obligation. We started with a conference that aligned everyone on what mattered. We then introduced them to the five leadership practices needed to shift the culture. These practices addressed Care,[34] Conversations for Action,[35] Reporting of Promises,[36] Managing Breakdowns,[37] and Creating Interdependencies.[38] These practices would enable change leaders to use their work to build the collaborative mindsets and routines needed to sustain the emerging collaborative culture.

BREAKDOWN: DISCOVERING SENIOR LEADERSHIP IS INDIFFERENT TO THE PROMISE

The first phase with senior leadership lasted five months: one month per practice. We soon saw that these executives showed little interest in changing the culture and in developing as leaders. Only 7 of the 24 even completed all five practices. The vice presidents who did participate succeeding in producing some change within their individual areas. However, these limited results were insufficient to accomplish culture shift for the whole bank.

It became apparent that the senior management group's commitment to modernization centered on the *president*, rather than the *organization*. As we heard from the group, "We don't know whether we will still be here in a year. If there's a change in the political regime, it's quite possible there will also be a change in organizational leadership, with no assurance we will still be in these roles." Because of this uncertainty, the vice presidents did not choose to commit to the company, its culture, or its future. The vice presidents saw their work as a fixed-term project—and didn't see the point of investing in leadership or building a culture for an organization to which they were not committed.

RECOVERING THE PROMISE
WITH PEOPLE WHO CARE

The lackluster engagement of the senior leadership team put the culture transformation in jeopardy. The sponsor team, led by the director of training, doubted whether to move forward after seeing the limited results of this first phase. I reminded the director of training of her vision: creating a future for the bank that aligned people across silos to build a better experience for employees and customers.

She wasn't the only one who cared about the bank. One of this company's fundamental assets was the employees' passion and the devotion they felt for the bank because of the difference the organization had made for lives and professional growth. When I asked people how long they had been there, their answer was fifteen, twenty, even twenty-five years. Many were proud to wear buttons on their lapels showing thirty years of service to the company. With this in mind, we decided to shift the attention of our change efforts to the people who managed the daily activities and kept the bank running.

The vice president of human capital, to whom the director of training reported, trusted our promise to accomplish the new culture and decided to let this initiative continue to a second phase. Our focus shifted towards taking care of the concerns and building the capacity of the people who would remain even if the country's political leadership changed.

ACHIEVING THE PROMISE

This second phase succeeded. Seventy-three percent of mid-level leaders joined the process with their teams early and voluntarily. The remaining leaders decided to join later, with encouragement from their peers. According to the adoption curve introduced by Everett Rogers,[39] we would expect to see half the early participation we experienced here.

Participants sustained their engagement through the end of the process and beyond. Nearly all the people (98%) who completed the five leadership practices declared satisfaction and created positive change in internal communications and business results. The directors who implemented the practices reported that their own leadership changed favorably and that their teams were working more cohesively and productively.

Positive changes emerged across the company. Leaders communicated more frequently and clearly. Frontline teams began to see their interdependencies more clearly and bridged silos across the bank. New teams formed to create innovative solutions for some of the bank's biggest challenges.

The success of this phase of the project allowed us to expand the culture initiative in four additional phases. We trained a group of high-potentials to become internal facilitators. These facilitators then trained more than 2,500 people directly and an additional 5,000 indirectly through managers and supervisors. The facilitator group has continued operating, and employees look forward to their turn to learn directly from these facilitators.

The five leadership pillars established during these several years allowed the organization to navigate VP-level leadership changes while sustaining a productive culture, fulfilling the promise of the project. The organization went from being composed of individuals who did tasks as ordered by management to being committed teams delivering on promises, supported by respected managers with professional standards for their work.

The bank has now designated a larger group of facilitators and with our help, they are now rolling out four additional practices to drive further leadership growth and innovation.

What enabled us to generate this kind of culture—without the support of upper management?

STARTING WITH CARE, VISION, AND COMMITMENT

One of the key elements of this process was the clear and committed care of the director of training. Although not in senior management, she thoroughly understood the organization and what could be achieved if the organization was correctly aligned and the people developed.

She had a vision that she knew could generate satisfaction, value, and meaning for the organization and its employees. She was personally committed to the productive future she knew was possible for the bank. This is what we call care in the discipline of generative leadership.[40]

The clarity of her vision—and her commitment to taking action to make this real—enabled the organization to bet on this culture project. They chose to create a culture based on the kind of leadership wanted by the most important asset of the bank: the people. People who had worked there for years felt this commitment and wanted to give back to the company that had supported them.

Leadership is the choice of people who point toward a vision and drive concrete and coordinated actions that generate results.

DEVELOPING COMMITTED LEADERS

The training director has since been promoted to become the bank's vice president of human capital. in this role, she ensures that the leadership project is taken to every corner of the country and the organization, allowing all levels to have clear communication and proven leadership practices. She personally committed to a three-year program to develop her own leadership.

Note that leadership is not a role: Leadership is the choice of people who point toward a vision and drive concrete and coordinated actions that generate results. Every organization has people who may not have titles or formal authority yet can inspire and engage others with the power of their conviction and actions.

These early leaders inspire people at all levels to share the valuable future they see for the company and take action to make it so. The more people in a company who share the future, and the more people eager and able to lead projects and teams, the faster, more fully, and more sustainably the company will innovate and accomplish results that matter to customers, employees, and other stakeholders.

CHANGING OUR COMPANY
STARTS WITH US

Diego Pose Galindo
FORMER GENERAL MANAGER, SOFTLAND PERÚ

In 2016, I took on the challenge of leading a software company that had been run for more than 20 years by its founder and now had been acquired by a multinational company.

We had many challenges ahead of us—building an environment of trust where there was none, mixing cultures, developing new lines of business, leading through breakdowns, and establishing new standards both in operations and communication. My initial reaction was to take it all on myself. The stress wore me down, and I lived with constant back pain and exhaustion.

I decided to seek a way of leading that would get results without crushing me or anyone else. As a step in this direction, I participated in the Generative Leadership Program which helped me see my assumptions about leadership. I asked myself what kind of leader I wanted to be and what future I wanted to build for this company. I realized I could accomplish this future only by inviting my team to build it with me. And I didn't need to wait for the whole company to change. We could start with our own operation.

This led to a radical change in my relationship with myself, my leadership, and my team. I became able to engage my team and change the company's culture—dealing productively with operational breakdowns, building new teams, and, above all, leading from a spirit of joy rather than contraction. As we created these changes in the company's Perú operations, we accomplished our goals—and inspired leaders in other areas of the company to strengthen their workplace culture.

TURNING CARE AND VISION INTO A SHARED PROMISE

Remember that as we started preparing the project, we discovered that the senior leadership training we were asked to provide would be insufficient to satisfy the organization's care. We needed a broader approach to address the concerns of the 65% of employees who were not satisfied with how the company operated but who felt powerless to generate change.

This culture initiative grew powerfully from the company's people, their love for the organization, and their desire to learn and grow in the place where many of them had worked since they were teenagers. Their commitment became to create a better place for people who loved the company and who had given and would give their best. At its center, the vision included the organization's people who wanted to do their best for each other and their customers.

When employees heard this vision for the future, they understood the shift proposed, and they realized that this culture change would address the ongoing silent pain that was seldom discussed across years of changing leadership at the top. Employee concerns, and the resignation they felt, would no longer be pushed to the side. Seeing that those who were driving change were also longtime workers made accomplishing the vision a commitment that employees across the bank could take to heart. We returned time and again to the care of the employees, and we centered on their shared promise.

Without relying on senior management, but with their permission, mid-level and frontline employees embraced practices to develop as leaders, invigorated their teams, expanded cross-unit collaboration, and accomplished the transformation of their company.

THE 3 LEVELS OF COMMITMENT

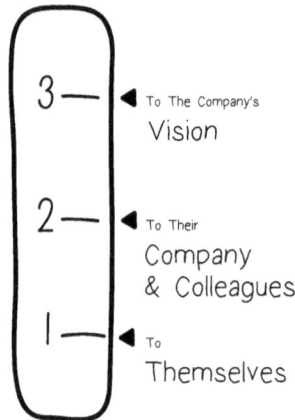

3 — ◀ To The Company's
Vision

2 — ◀ To Their
Company
& Colleagues

1 — ◀ To
Themselves

BUILDING AND SUSTAINING THE CHANGE TEAM

The same factors that enabled the cultural change—ongoing care for the employees and the organization, a shared vision, and personal commitment to accomplishing it—were essential to forming and sustaining the team of facilitators.

When we started working with the bank, the company was in the process of modernization, and numerous projects were already under way. Accordingly, people were busy, yet many wanted to join the facilitation team. They knew that the bank needed a new culture and that it needed to work for everyone. With this broad interest, we formed a team of people from all levels of the organization.

We knew it would be essential to create a
sense of belonging and real support.

Prospective facilitators knew this wouldn't be easy. When facilitators decided to join the team, they committed to a rigorous training program and the promise of reaching out to 8,000 employees while continuing to do their regular jobs at the bank. Given double-duty in their jobs and the ambition of the team's promise, we knew it would be essential to create a sense of belonging and real support.

Members of the change and facilitation teams told us these elements were key to their satisfying experience on this challenging project:

- **The request from leadership was clear from the start.** Each individual voluntarily decided to accept the commitment and conditions of satisfaction of the promise. These conditions were clear and specific from the beginning.

- **Team members were inspired by each other and the project.** Each felt it was up to them to own the responsibility for creating a culture where everyone could be a leader. They saw that this change was needed and were convinced it was possible.

- **They liked belonging to a team where everyone was committed to accomplishing the promise and to working efficiently.** They operated with high standards and aimed for impeccable coordination. Members reminded each other when they saw commitment flagging. In their team, they used the practices and language they taught the company. Together they vetted ideas, tested designs, navigated breakdowns, and stayed focused on their promise to the company.

- **They had a clear mission.** Every person was able to articulate the mission and knew what they had to do to achieve it.

- **Leadership recognized their work.** Recognition started with this team's leader and over the course of the project recognition increased throughout the company. Many people across the organization appreciated these team members, recognizing each for their personal contribution.

- **Their customer was as committed as they were.** The director of training's commitment matched those of the team. She did not act as though the project was primarily hers; instead, she functioned as an integral part of the team. She accompanied, guided, nurtured, and trusted them, and she highlighted the value of their work. She also managed the team efficiently; communication was constant, clear, and useful.

- **Belonging to a successful team was rewarding.** Without changing roles or getting promotions, team members could be part of this "elite" team of people who were changing the organization. This gave them meaning and satisfaction that they had not felt previously. Each team member felt proud to be part of this visible, transformative project.

- **Everyone focused on the promise in ways that nurtured the team.** Each person who had been part of the promise continued to support the project. The leader gave ongoing visibility and continuity. The project manager, the champions, the facilitators—and even the consultant—continued to feed a promise that belonged to everyone. This made a cohesive and aligned team in which everyone was proud to participate.

With these factors in place, team members felt seen, developed, valuable, and fulfilled. They saw how their actions gave more meaning and value to their careers, more joy to their work together, and a new future to the whole organization. An internal climate survey of the beginning of the project showed that only 63% of employees rated company leadership as effective; three years into the project, 95% rated their leaders as effective. Absenteeism went down substantially, and the bank was recognized with a Great Place to Work award.

The bank was successful in modernizing critical processes, which many believe wouldn't have been possible without this culture shift. Nearly a decade later, the bank continues to develop every person in the company at all levels in the five practices.

Together with this team, across these five years of work, we developed transformational relationships with enduring mutual commitment.

In this project, I learned that it's possible to build the thriving organizations we seek as consultants. What was needed was to set aside the general wisdom to start with the most senior team and instead look for the people who cared and were most willing to commit to growing and to create a new future.

In generative leadership, we put people and what they care about at the center of the game. In this way, we create teams and ultimately organizations with people who are "alive"—who are energized, dedicated, ready to learn, committed to the promise, and focused on doing the work to fulfill that promise.

Business results come from these teams of people—from people who know what they care about, commit to creating a better future, face the challenges that arise together, and sustain each other on the journey.

RECOMMENDED ACTIONS

- **Start with and regularly review what the team cares about.**
  Where do they see the need for change and evolution? Invite
  senior leaders to do this with their teams and share the results.
  Hold a care conversation at least three times per year.

- **Listen for the values and moods of your employees.**
  Understand what people treasure about being part of the
  company and what makes them feel proud to be in the
  organization. Reinforcing these values should become part of the
  habits of the company.

- **Listen for commitment at each level of the organization.**
  Every person in the company needs three levels of commitment:

  - To themselves: Always aiming to learn, to seek feedback,
    and working at their learning edge to accelerate their
    development.

  - To their team and other people in the company: Engaging
    in sometimes uncomfortable conversations to build truly a
    truly aligned organization.

  - To the company's vision: Which will deliver value to their
    customers and communities.

WHEN THE TEAM YOU NEED DOESN'T EXIST

Jan Irene Miller

- What do you do when you make a promise you can't fulfill with people who report to you?

- How will you gain and blend the skills and commitments of people in distinct locations and cultures?

- How might you involve the people who will have to live with the results of your work?

In 2012, my husband and I were living in South Africa, and I went to visit friends in a small village in Zambia. The 1500 people of the local tribe lived simply in modest, traditional dwellings—without electricity, running water, or sewer systems. The Zambian government operated a school and clinic, which had become important community gathering places. However, with no electricity to relieve the intense heat, it was hard to keep enough teachers and nurses, and the buildings were usable for only a few hours each day.

My friends presented me with a challenge: "We've tried for seven years to get the electricity extended from the nearest station without success. Will you help us bring electricity to the village?"

HANDLING A CHALLENGE OUTSIDE
YOUR WHEELHOUSE

Let's say you've been invited to make something happen, and you don't know what that will entail. All you know is it will involve more than what you can accomplish with your skills and network alone. This invitation could come from a department within your organization but beyond your functional expertise, such as moving from product design to marketing or distribution. The ask could be to take on a new initiative. Or, as was my experience in Zambia, you might be asked to lead an unfamiliar project in an unfamiliar place—harnessing the skills of people you don't yet know.

Because of my limited knowledge of the local culture and language, I wasn't sure I could assemble and manage a local team dedicated to this project. The leader on this project would need to generate a network of trustworthy commitments for an array of roles, responsibilities, and skills not yet known. Some of the commitments would have to come from the community, and others from governmental and commercial organizations that authorize and build electrical infrastructure. Whom could I trust? I didn't have this network in Zambia.

The task ahead seemed impossibly messy, complicated, risky, and intense. It would be rewarding if it succeeded, and potentially damaging and dangerous if it failed.

In your work, how do you do something you've never done before? How do you act and step into that unknown—rather than feeling like you have to know everything before you act? And how do you build a successful team that will walk into the unknown with you?

This was not an entirely new situation for me. Having led matrixed teams for Silicon Graphics and Atos Origin at their peaks of innovation, and having pulled together seemingly impossible projects in Chile and Panama, I knew to take a breath and explore the terrain before (or better yet, instead of) panicking. I remained open and let myself relax into the conversation. I knew at least I could explore the situation and figure out how we might move forward before making a commitment to the project. I continued listening with curiosity for the possibilities and the intention of their request.

CREATING A TEAM THAT DOESN'T EXIST

I first asked people to tell me what they'd tried so far. This is a prospective team leader's way of getting grounded in the context—including the background and history of previous conversations—to determine where the roadblocks and frustrations were and who might be the right people to become part of the solution.

I was being asked to produce an outcome that needed a team that didn't exist and that I couldn't manage directly. In this situation, where there were clearly many risks, previous barriers, and challenges, it would take multiple conversations to assess the feasibility of the request. Then, if I could commit to accomplishing it, we would need to create a matrix-managed team across multiple organizations and geographies to succeed.

Like other teams, a matrix-managed team requires the ability to produce multi-stakeholder value. This sort of team requires a network of commitments toward a common promise. The team leader must navigate the layers of authority from contributors and their bosses to secure the commitment necessary to produce the desired result. Securing trustworthy agreements and coordinating the action to fulfill those agreements is key to successful outcomes and can be especially tricky when the people do not directly report to you. They have another boss, and with that management structure comes another set of commitments and priorities.

The leader of a matrix-managed team acts as both the glue and the choreographer for the network of teams working on his or her behalf.

In a matrix-managed team, the leader acts as both the glue and the choreographer for the network of people and teams working to accomplish the result. This sort of team is similar to other teams in that there is an end game, and all the players are making promises to fulfill their part. The difference is that each of the players is not necessarily committed to the success of all the others. The accountability for the desired end result lies more with the overall team leader and her ability to negotiate with other leaders, secure reliable promises from them, and effectively manage a wide array of commitments.

What is possible in a matrix-managed team that is well coordinated by the team leader—especially one that may need to operate remotely and serve multiple stakeholders from multiple cultures?

- Such a team provides an opportunity for equity, diversity, and inclusion across cultures and professions.
- It gives people a chance to contribute and be included in the sweet spot of their skills.

- It provides opportunities for creative, ambitious learners to be involved in unique challenges building engagement and loyalty in an organization.

- It involves a series of small asks from many individuals, which make lighter work for all.

- When all stakeholders have a voice, they can produce sustainable results.

- Managed well, these teams can act with agility and effectiveness, sharing costs and burdens across a broader spectrum.

- Matrix-managed teams can save time and money, compared to hiring and building a direct team to take on special projects, key strategic initiatives, or process improvement.

In this case, I needed to understand not only the technological and financial feasibility of the project, but also the authority, power, and politics of the situation. The context of the overlapping national, ministerial, civil, and tribal jurisdictions would be in play. Politics, egos, motivations, and intentions must be understood and included. What did we know about their cares and concerns? How could we secure the trust and cooperation of the players in the surrounding organizations, institutions, and government structures?

When you can be open, present, and connected in a conversation, listen to the cares and concerns of the other person, and explore a place of mutual interest and care, it's usually possible to find a way to move forward into the next conversation. Because each person listens according to their cultural history and embodied, practiced behaviors, it's always important to have that history or to have someone with you who can support you in understanding how people listen and navigate conversations.[41] This is not unique to any state, province, or country. You may find yourself being asked to lead a team that has an existing history that shapes their relationships and their attitude towards you. You'll find it essential to listen for their cultural history, values, relationships, and acceptable behaviors, as these impact what you can do together.

WHAT MIGHT THIS PROJECT ACCOMPLISH?

Without knowing the villagers' culture, capabilities, and goals, I entered the conversation with curiosity. I wondered what might be possible for this project and what vision the villagers had for the future. Among the goals they shared for bringing electricity to the village were:

- Attracting and keeping teachers
- Improving the quality of education so that more of the village's children qualify to enter the high school in the city and graduate
- Better sanitation and community health
- Evening classes for young parents who want to continue their learning, so that they can understand the lessons and be of more assistance to their children
- Ability to offer home economics and computer skills
- The option for adults to learn to read and write to be informed voters
- An evening classroom gathering space for teenagers searching for safe places to talk, study, or play together

- Improved, expanded, and more consistent healthcare programs, including refrigeration for regular vaccinations
- A community gathering space for discussing tribal business

From these initial conversations, I began to understand the possibilities that electricity might create. Subsequent gatherings allowed attendees to share their thoughts about what this project meant to them.

Have you sped forward with a proposal, only to find that some of the constituents didn't agree or feel they had ownership of the plan? Generating engagement is not a one-time conversation; it's a process of connection, exploration, and relationship building. What does it take for people to get engaged and care about a particular outcome?

Generating engagement is not a one-time conversation; it's a process of connection, exploration, and relationship building.

For engagement, cooperation, and to fulfill the broadest possibility of the project, it's important to explore the cares and concerns of those most impacted by this change. You've probably been in a family, community, or organizational situation where this didn't happen—where a change "announced" without your input created resistance and distrust.

Listening engages people in the project and allows you to design solutions aligned with the desires of those most impacted by the change. It also opens the door for sharing new and innovative ideas. When people know they have been heard, they are more open to other people's ideas and priorities.

PARTNERSHIPS NEED SHARED VISION AND ACCOUNTABILITY

Jason L. Kessler

PROGRAM EXECUTIVE SMALL BUSINESS INNOVATION RESEARCH & SMALL BUSINESS TECHNOLOGY TRANSFER PROGRAM, NASA

In 2010, I joined a high-profile National Aeronautics and Space Administration (NASA) team, amid an expansion. This initiative required a complex mix of new people, technology choices, and funding from two government agencies—each with its own culture, expectations, and needs. I was comfortable working in the NASA context but didn't have specific domain expertise or experience working with the other agency.

I was fortunate in that we brought in Jan Irene Miller, who had me stop and take a breath. She helped me realize I didn't have to have the answers—my job was to create a forum for experts to collaborate and share their ideas on navigating this new future. I guided the team to develop a shared understanding of what we were creating and to hold them accountable for their commitments. I also made time to connect with our partners at the other agency to understand their cares and concerns and to develop a shared language.

With Jan Irene's help, I learned to listen for people's care and commitment and to handle the inevitable breakdowns with grace and compassion. With this approach, I led our team to redefine the working relationship between the two agencies. This program now collaborates with over 250 institutions in forty-five countries, and enables more than 3,000 individuals to use earth science data more effectively to address the local challenges of climate change.

From my history of leading international projects, I knew to lead with curiosity rather than any sense that I had the answers. Here are questions I raised for the Zambian project:

Leadership:

- Who accepts overall accountability for the project?
- Who has the authority and could be trusted to manage on the ground in the village?
- How will villagers be included? How will we ensure they understand and own their role?

Technology and equipment:

- Are the technology and equipment available and accessible? In what timeframe?

Expertise:

- What kind of expertise is needed for this project?
- Are the expertise, capability, and capacity available?

Power and politics:

- What is the level of cooperation and coordination between the Tribal/Civil authorities?
- What power and political dynamics could derail or accelerate the project?
- What other key stakeholders have a say in the project?

Money/financial administration:

- What types of transparency, security, capabilities, and legalities exist for banking, money transfers and management, contracts, cash, and bookkeeping?
- Where is the money coming from?

Safety:

- What could protect or endanger workers, villagers, and stakeholders?
- How will workers mitigate physical dangers, environmental hazards, and theft/robbery?

Time:

- How might time zone coordination impact this project?
- Can this project be done before a key milestone—here, the start of school?
- What is the cultural relationship with time? How do we define terms like "soon" across cultures?

Culture:

- What does "yes" mean in this culture? Are people allowed to say "no" or "I don't know?" Are they comfortable with "figuring things out?"
- What are the long-term implications of this project? Is the village prepared to deal with such factors as lights and noise?

Sustainability:

- How will this project be maintained in the future? What will sustain it? Who will pay for the electricity? Who will maintain the equipment?
- What will be the unanticipated downsides and upsides of this project?
- Does this make sense in the scope of geography, politics, and economy?

ESTABLISHING CREDIBILITY

Within five months, I'd made my initial assessments of the project's feasibility and had begun to articulate the roles, responsibilities, and network of commitments necessary to fulfill the work before I agreed to go "all in."

I've learned that whenever I've been asked to accomplish an outcome without a dedicated team, I had to have a trustworthy identity and authority to start generating the network of commitments needed to get the job done. Otherwise, I'd likely hear, "That's not one of my priorities." Or, "My team doesn't have the capacity to help you." Or, "I wasn't informed my team would be needed for this." Or, "We've always done it this way." Or even, "I don't know you, and I don't work for you."

Having lived, consulted, and employed residents of South Africa for two years, I'd been learning about power dynamics between the races. This was invaluable to me in understanding how to engage in Zambia. I knew that other white people (such as tourist missionaries) had come many times to this area, and, with the best of intentions, left poorly constructed and unsustainable projects. To avoid the possibility that this project would suffer the same fate, I wanted to make sure this would be seen as belonging to the stakeholders, rather than to an English-speaking white woman. The innovator and trusted village leader needed to be the leader; my role was to be the person who supported her role and authority.

We gathered in the school so that, pictorially, with the help of a translator, I could draw the narrative arc of our relationships and further explore my requests of the stakeholders. I wanted to be clear about what I was willing to do in my role and to outline the support the local leader would require to complete the project. I clarified that there will be no project if this was not *your* project. We had open conversations to take care of what community members cared about. This included figuring out who would make sure the children were safe during the work, and who would attend to the food and water for the workers.

CREATING A MATRIX TEAM

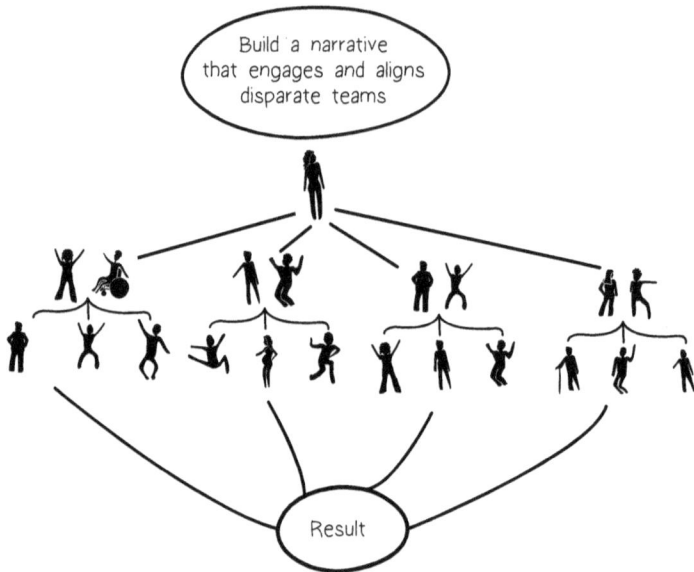

WHO AND WHAT IS NEEDED
TO PRODUCE THE RESULT?

From this listening, I confirmed that a matrix team with many different skill sets would be needed to provide the intended value for the community. To start, it would be my role to determine whether the project was feasible, whether it was coherent with the desired future of these people, and whether it made sense in the context and ecosystem of the area.

Before you agree to lead key strategic initiatives or special projects, you'll want to conduct a feasibility and sustainability assessment. Who needs to be on board to mitigate the risks? Who is on board now? What authority do I have and by whom is it granted? Who could possibly derail this? Is this feasible? Is it sustainable? And, in this case, does the project make sense geophysically and geopolitically?

After many conversations with friends and advisors and several months of feasibility and sustainability research regarding development in Africa, I made my initial assessment to continue forward.

Leaders don't have all the answers and cannot be expert in every domain of expertise involved in a project.

When you get an invitation for an exciting challenge, it's important to step back and take a deep breath. Get clear about the destination. You may be asked to lead a program, but what success looks like is not clearly articulated, the budget is not designated, and it's unclear whether this is even on anyone's radar.

The ability to make grounded assessment[42] and assess whether someone else is making valuable assessments may be one of the most important skills needed to lead a successful team.[43] This is especially important when you don't have a long history with the people you are leading and have only a short period to deliver results. Leaders don't have all the answers and cannot be expert in every domain of expertise involved in a project.

As a team leader, you must also assess the trustworthiness of potential team members' commitments and their competency to deliver on their promises. So many times, I've heard team leaders say, "They had ten years of experience, but I found that they still couldn't do the job."

Experience is an assessment of time, not competence in a particular domain of action. **Competence** is the ability to act effectively and recurrently in a specific domain of action.[44] It is observable, and, therefore, verifiable by you and by others. Leaders need to be able to listen to many different experts, offer their assessments of particular concerns, then navigate and share assessments until they are prepared to make informed decisions.

THE RESULT

In May 2013, the ribbon-cutting celebration at the village was attended by all the villagers, the tribal chief, and the civil authorities of the nearby town. Tents were raised, signs were posted, and costumed dancers performed. Music and songs played late into the night, and food was prepared for all. The event was televised and widely praised as an important milestone in the village's history, with deep appreciation from all stakeholders.

That day, I felt incredible relief and gratitude that the project was complete. It had been accomplished within a year—just weeks before I was to move back to the United States. The relief came from knowing the project had been completed successfully without physical harm to anyone. While there were many risks, safety was always on my mind in the face of the hazards in this remote location and the presence of villagers—especially children—during the installation of the telephone poles, lines, transformer, and wiring. The village also had clear plans and commitments for maintaining what they had created.

Relying on the promises of others takes faith, not just skill, and in this case, I leaned on my faith. On the day when I participated in the beautiful surprises of the celebration, side-by-side with local leaders, I felt deep satisfaction from playing an improbable role in bringing forth the rich capability of this community to produce outcomes that matter.

RECOMMENDED ACTIONS IN ESTABLISHING A MATRIX TEAM

- **Create a narrative** that engages the people (organizations, institutions, municipalities, consultants, etc.) from whom you will draw your needed expertise with the result you intend to create together.

  - Start by saying yes to exploring the situation, rather than yes to the project.

  - Determine what competencies are needed, where you can find those people, and the tools, equipment, and resources they will need.

  - Connect with the leaders of existing teams who may engage with the project.

  - Listen to their interests and concerns and take these into consideration.

  - Make your requests for help (people, process, and action) and negotiate trustworthy promises.

- **Address questions of authority.**

  - Be clear about who will authorize the project and what power you will have to drive outcomes.

  - Clarify with the individuals involved that you, as the team leader, have the authority to lead, in service of accomplishing the outcomes. Negotiate the conditions of participation for their team members.

-   Make sure the agreements of each person on the team will add up to accomplishing the overall promise.

- **Keep the team coordinated** and focused on accomplishing the outcome.

    -   Set up a regular rhythm of conversation, so everyone starts and stays on the same page with commitments, changing priorities, and project status.

    -   Respect the work of each participant in building the project's success, and celebrate achieving milestones and results!

SECTION TWO

MAKING TEAMS AMAZING

EVERY TEAM IS A PROMISE

Sameer Dua

- What promise does your team exist to fulfill?

- Can the company trust your team to deliver on that promise?

- Do the promises of teams across the organization add up to your company's promise to customers and investors?

The Chief Financial Officer (CFO) landed a big opportunity, and he was ambitious to make the most of it.

For at least the next two months until the new CEO arrived, he was the acting CEO of his large business unit. This CFO, let's call him Rahm, knew this was his chance to be seen across the global company as a candidate for corporate CEO. Rahm decided to call his functional heads together for a Management Review. He wanted to get a read on the business, make sure the departments were functioning well, and start a monthly pattern of reporting status. He asked me to come and observe.

In this meeting, each department head spoke about the actions their group had taken in the last month and what they probably should do in the following month. They did not discuss what their department had committed to accomplishing, nor did they show progress against those commitments. They did not offer support for cross-functional processes, nor did they make requests of other departments.

I noticed the department heads spoke in a language of "thoughts and plans" and sometimes "concerns and complaints." Their peers nodded in response. For example, there were many complaints about quality, and the quality leader nodded politely. But he was only nodding that he shared the concern—he made no promise to resolve the problem. And no one, including Rahm, asked him to do anything differently. A few people appeared delighted they had "communicated" their problems to the distressed departments. Yet it was evident from looking at the faces and body language of these leaders that there was no commitment to do anything differently in the following month.

Additionally, two management team members did not show up to the meeting. They sent their deputies, who were at a disadvantage for two reasons. First, the deputies did not understand what their bosses had promised, so they couldn't report effectively on status. Second, it seemed they were not given the authority to make further promises to align their departments with others. So, these two representatives simply nodded and took notes.

Then, one team lead started to speak about targets, why they hadn't accomplished them, and how it was acceptable not to meet monthly targets. The room did not respond. For a moment, I stepped out of my observer role and asked this team lead whether that target was his promise. He said no. It wasn't a promise—just a target. When I asked what the difference was, he said, "I guess we promised that we would try to do it, but not that we would make it happen."

There was equal nonchalance about fulfilling the overall business promise to customers. Everyone seemed to believe the business was not doing well, but no one was willing to say that out loud. It was also evident that they did not trust other team members to deliver as intended. The mood of the meeting was resignation: we don't expect anything to get better, and we don't see we can do anything about it. No one said or did anything to discuss or shift that perception.

That two-hour meeting showed what was missing. These management team members were not focused on the company's promise to customers. Furthermore, they did not know what was needed from their various functions to fulfill even a rather sloppy version of what the customer expected. They weren't clear on the promises they had made for their own departments nor what they needed from each other.

Rahm, the acting CEO with big dreams for his career, accepted what the others said as if he heard promises, rather than vague plans and empty targets. Rahm also missed the necessary behaviors of what we call "an effective customer": inviting rigor about who will accomplish what by when to what standard.[45] He continued to call them a management "team" without insisting they share a promise to customers nor coordinate to deliver that promise.

PROMISES CREATE TEAMS

Here's what I shared with Rahm after the session:

A promise is your commitment to producing a certain kind of future. When you make a promise, you become responsible for producing that future. In some cases, that future is very specific, e.g., I promise our company will have a new factory the size of our existing factory operational within 10 months. Or, I promise our external quality audit will place us in the upper third of our industry by next September. In some cases, the promise is directional, e.g., I promise our work-from-home practices will stay compliant with local laws as they change.

Teams are set up to fulfill promises.
No promise, no team.

Teams are set up to fulfill promises. More precisely, a shared promise is the act that creates the team. No promise, no team.[46]

Furthermore, the identity of the team is dependent on the promises that it makes and how it manages those promises. If a team makes a promise that is not big enough or does not address what matters to the organization, that team becomes known as irrelevant. If a team makes a relevant promise but does not effectively manage it—they don't update the specifics of their promise when conditions change, they don't coordinate delivery with other teams, etc.—then this team is viewed as untrustworthy, poorly run, and a drag on the business.

Look around your own company. You'll see the teams that you re-spect make promises that ensure the organization succeeds in ad-dressing what matters most. You'll see that these teams are fulfilling their commitments. On the rare occasions that they cannot fulfill commitments, they're effectively managing them by revoking or re-negotiating early.

A note about how we define a promise: a *promise* is a declarative act[47] we make which organizes us to be in action for the sake of produc-ing a specific outcome. It is also an act communicated beyond our team to produce an understanding in others of why we exist and how valuable we are to the company. Furthermore, promises are acts of coordination between people.

WHAT'S AT STAKE

I think about the impact of managing or not managing promises as the four R's. What's at stake is our **Reputation, Results, Relation-ships**, and **self-Respect**. In my book *Become*,[48] I focused on the indi-vidual leader, but clearly these four factors are as relevant for teams. Teams that fail to make, fulfill, or manage promises suffer a poor reputation, produce substandard results, and damage relationships in the team and across the company.

Poor promise-keeping also profoundly damages team members' self-respect and agency. When the head of quality on Rahm's team returned to his department after that meeting, do you think he greeted them with determination and ambition for the next month? I suspect he slouched back to the department, muttered that the com-pany doesn't understand quality, told them to try to work harder, and closed his door. Did his people then pull together, lean forward, re-mind each other how capable they are individually and together, and develop better ways to deliver quality to the business? I doubt that.

Gaps in making and fulfilling promises tend to erode team members' respect for each other and themselves, which in turn drives a downward spiral in performance. Conversely, making and keeping promises elevates reputations, builds relationships, increases self-respect, and puts your team on track for better results—all of which give your organization and customers the confidence to trust you with bigger promises.

YOUR COMPANY IS A NETWORK OF PROMISES

An organization exists to fulfill bigger commitments than could any individual. At the start, the organization may be one team that commits to creating the future of the organization. As the organization grows, we see that smaller groups of people can best take care of focused promises that nest within the overall commitment of the organization. Teams form when a group of people agrees to hold a promise together and to coordinate their actions to fulfill it.

You now have an entire organization—
not primarily of roles, but of promises.

We can see any organization as a network of promises.[49]

The CEO or Managing Director makes the organization's promise in consultation with leaders of businesses, functions, and initiatives. The CEO has been granted the authority by its shareholders, through its board, to declare what the company will accomplish. This leader then needs to ensure that promises from the heads of functions and business units add up to the overall commitment of the company.

The leader of a business unit or function is the person coordinating—internally and externally—by making these promises and then effectively managing them. The leader must ensure that the entire team is committed. If not, this will lead to dissatisfaction and a low likelihood of success.

These leaders and teams also make requests of adjacent teams to coordinate, so that together they can fulfill promises. In effective organizations, teams take responsibility for coordinating well with other teams. This cycle of promises and responsibility continues.

You now have an entire organization—not primarily of roles, but of promises.

A TARGET OR A PROMISE?

We regularly ask, is this a target or a promise? The response we normally hear is, "Oh, it's a target. I'm not promising I can hit it." Many people see a target as something they should attempt to complete, but if they don't achieve it, that's just how it worked out. A target is essentially a request made by the manager to a performer to create specific outcomes. It's just a request until the performer makes a promise: "This is my promise, and I *will* achieve it."

Several organizations I have worked with have stopped using targets. They now have decided to operate from promises of results from their team members. This is not just a matter of semantics. This is a matter of how team members show up to work every morning—committed to achieving a result.

Sometimes we make promises that we know we can achieve. Other times, we make a promise to do something new or particularly challenging—trusting our capacity to learn, create, navigate breakdowns, and make it happen. At other times, we see that our resources (including creativity, energy, adaptability, and power) are insufficient to make a certain promise.[50] I cannot, for example, make a trustworthy promise to get myself to the moon tomorrow. Yet, thoughtful "moonshots" can succeed because they organize teams to bring enormous resources and innovative practices to fulfill an inspiring promise.

Tasks don't produce value—results do.

Often, team members accept impossible targets fearing they cannot negotiate or decline what's been dropped onto them by their manager. Indeed, I've heard many managers say they want to hear "Yes!" to any request they make. But what if the real answer is "No"? When would you want to know they won't deliver—now while you're talking or the day before the client meeting?

You can think of it this way: when someone declines what they've been asked to take on, could it be that person is saying they care about team performance and don't want to let you down? Since the person you asked does not have the capacity, competence, or the intention to do what you're asking them to do, they won't accept the responsibility. This allows you to find another way to create the result you had in mind. Of course, if team members regularly don't have the capacity, competence, or intention to perform, that points you toward a different set of conversations.

As a leader or fellow team member, you want more than your colleague's rapid "Yes" to take on the task. You want them to own accomplishing the result. Tasks don't produce value—results do. So, you both need to be clear on the results that will satisfy you—on behalf of the team, the company, and ultimately the purchaser of your goods or services.

CLEAR PROMISES POWERED OUR TURNAROUND

Rohit Kumar
COO, SIEMENS ADVANTA DEVELOPMENT

A vague intent to perform well doesn't mean much. However, a clear and specific promise has a totally different impact. As such promises stack up across an organization, amazing things happen.

I once took over an under-performing business—one with increasing costs, no growth, and high attrition. This was an experienced team, but somehow the business was falling apart. Conversations with people at all levels revealed that they weren't clear what they could expect from each other. Everyone had a target, such as lowering attrition. Yet, no one was promising anything to anyone.

I firmly believed that we as a business could do much better. Working with Sameer, I discovered two powerful steps to turn this around:

- I needed to state my promise publicly and clearly: *I am going to grow this business 10% year-over-year, and I commit to removing every hurdle that stops you from innovating.*

- I needed to invite others to question my promise so they understood that I truly meant what I said.

Once enough people understood my promise, I asked them how *they* would make us successful. It took time for them to make their promises, but steadily things began to come together: the rookie engineer promised to build the first augmented reality prototype; the business development manager promised to grow at least five customers per quarter; the team manager promised to reduce effort waste by 10%.

Performance on all metrics improved. We grew by 15%, our attrition dropped, and some of our earlier stars even came back to the team.

This is not rocket science. It's simply about what you commit to achieve and why these promises matter—to the organization, to the teams involved, and, most importantly, to yourself.

USE PROMISES TO DRIVE CLARITY

When a promise is made, there are always two interpretations of what it means: one in the eye of the Performer (the person who makes the promise) and another in the eye of the Customer (the person to whom the promise is made).[51] Unless these interpretations match, the organization will be out of alignment.

Effective promises include what we call the Conditions of Satisfaction— a clear description of the standards of the outcome that will satisfy the Customer.[52] For example, if I ask a team member for a promise to create a welcome video for new hires, both of us need to be clear on the criteria for declaring the promise fulfilled. With those standards mutually understood, the Performer (here, my colleague) can choose to make a trustworthy promise, and I am likely to be satisfied with the result.

Let's look at the example of another large public company—a 140-year-old company with revenues of about $70 billion annually. In 2017, as they were in a fight to sustain market share, I worked with the managing director, their leadership team, and their entire sales team of 2000 people.

We made one change: we got everyone focused on asking for and making effective promises.

No longer did they act as if a target handed to them by their boss represented just the boss's request. The new standard was to ask the salespeople and other leaders what they promised to deliver. Because people at all levels came to focus on how to make promises trustworthy (rather than just nod yes and hope they can hit targets), they became able to manage and fulfill these promises. As a result, they achieved unprecedented 40% year-over-year sales growth.

We also helped this company move from a chart of functions and titles to an organization chart of promises. Each team held an explicit promise with Conditions of Satisfaction that everyone understood. With this clarity, people were able to coordinate rapidly and effectively across functions to deliver the product to their growing customer base.

Your impact on the world is a function of the value and size of your promises and how well you deliver on them.

START WITH YOU

As a leader or team member, only make promises for which you can commit to delivering. If you think you cannot live up to a promise, decline and negotiate for a result that you and your team can produce. If at a later point, you realize that you cannot honor a promise you've made, revoke or renegotiate it as soon as possible. Keep your team's promises clear and current, so your team stays aligned with adjacent teams and customers.

Finally, I invite you to notice: *you* are a promise. Your impact on the world is a function of the value and size of your promises and how well you deliver on them.

RECOMMENDED ACTIONS

- **Ask each member of your team to jot down the promise of the team.** Then, ask your team's sponsor, business leader or CEO, and the leaders of your upstream and downstream teams. If you hear different answers, go have the conversations to align on a valuable promise your team can deliver.

- **Ask to what extent the promise is trustworthy.** How might you work together to ensure you deliver? Understand what does and doesn't make your output valuable to the customer, how to match team output and capacity, and how to create a rhythm of communication with adjacent teams so that you can deliver together.

- **Map your organization as a network of promises.** Work with senior leaders to put a map on the wall and determine where promises are coherent and where there are gaps.

- **Strengthen your ability as a leader to detect trustworthy promises in others.** Listen not only to the words being spoken but also to the mood you see on faces and in body language.

    - Make your promises trustworthy.

    - Commit to keeping all your promises.

    - Make only those promises that you can keep.

    - If in the event you cannot deliver, revoke or renegotiate that promise and offer another way to take care of what matters to your organization and customers.

RESPONSIBILITY TRANSFORMS TEAMS

Juliana Vergara

- How do responsibility and accountability show up in teams?

- Do you hear complaints, excuses, or silence in your meetings?

- What can you do to cultivate responsibility in yourself and others?

Two different organizations engaged me to help improve their leadership teams.

Max, the CEO of the first company, told me, "I need a team that's ready for the future, and I suspect few of my current execs will make it." I wondered what he meant by that, since the team had great experience. "I have an open door policy," he continued. "People are welcome to bring ideas anytime—but they don't. I see no initiative or creativity. In meetings, they sit silently, waiting for me to make decisions. I'm shouldering all the responsibility for the company's future, and I don't see them stepping up to help."

The second organization was quite a contrast. People were very vocal in meetings, with a continuous stream of blame and excuses for unmet expectations. The negativity was contagious—just walking in the door, I could feel moods of resentment and frustration. The CEO of this organization, Mike, felt utterly alone amid the barrage: "I want to listen to them and engage them in improving, but all I hear is negativity. I believe in the product, but I might need to swap out the whole team."

At first glance, these two companies had completely different leadership challenges. One organization was entirely passive, while the other was vocal and combative. You'd think the interventions needed would have been quite different.

However, as I began to coach the CEOs and executive teams, I realized that the problems at both companies stemmed from the same root: team members who didn't choose responsibility.

In both companies, people looked to others to resolve problems they experienced. They neither brought suggestions nor made requests or offers to help. These teams had something else in common: The team members were more committed to being seen as right or blameless than getting product to market. Unsurprisingly, both Max and Mike felt frustrated, lonely, and unsure how to proceed.

A CHOICE OF OPERATING SYSTEMS: BEING A VICTIM OR BEING RESPONSIBLE

Leaders must identify the invisible operating systems that underlie culture if they are to intervene effectively in their organizations. These operating systems represent the lens through which team members perceive themselves, others, and the world. Rewiring an operating system is possible but requires awareness, choice, and practice.

One key aspect of the operating system is whether your team adopts a posture of responsibility or victimhood. Posture refers to a readiness to act in a certain way. In some companies, people come to work prepared to take action to fulfill promises made to customers. In others, people come ready to blame or hide.

---

*People taking the posture
of responsibility choose to build
a future that matters to them.*

The Me/We/World framework, introduced in the *Foundations* chapter, can help us understand the contrasting mindsets and behaviors we see in victims relative to responsible team members.

The ME space highlights how we see ourselves and interpret the situations around us.

People in a **victim** mindset believe they cannot significantly impact their future. They may live from a story of feeling incapable, unheard, or unsupported. They embody a mood of resignation. Some victims express themselves vocally with emotional outbursts, while others prefer to stay passive and let others determine their fate. Since other people tend to respond unsupportively, victims easily become trapped in cycles of excuses, blame, frustration, avoidance, drama, and disengagement.

On the other hand, people taking the posture of **responsibility** choose to build a future that matters to them. They act from a mindset of seeing possibilities and looking for ways to use their strengths and networks to accomplish results. They embody moods of possibility, determination, and positive ambition. They make offers and promises they intend to fulfill, even as they face difficulties, and they design and redesign their approaches, learning as they go.

The WE space encompasses the interactions we share with others.

Victims often believe they must work alone to ensure success. They tend to blame others for miscommunication. By resisting feedback, they miss out on growth, and they inadvertently foster distrust. Victims may also be passive—avoiding risk and relying on others to make decisions for them. On teams, they prioritize being seen as right and avoiding conflict, which reduces the shared learning that is essential for teams to perform, improve, and innovate.

Responsible players, however, embrace collaboration. They recognize that their teams can fulfill bigger promises than if they were to work alone. They cultivate mutually beneficial relationships and appreciate feedback as a growth opportunity. By admitting their mistakes, learning from them, and seeking help, they create more significant opportunities for everyone. On teams, they seek opportunities to create value for their customers and help their colleagues grow, succeed, and increase their value to the organization.

The WORLD space is where your team delivers value.

In this realm, **victims** see life as something that happens to them. They feel at the mercy of circumstances and feel powerless against external circumstances. They view circumstances as a matter of luck or control by more powerful forces. This perspective hinders their ability to contribute positively to their organizations and communities.

Conversely, people in a posture of **responsibility** strive to create the change they wish to see in the world. They make commitments with others, and they navigate ambiguity so they can innovate together. Energized by collective ambition, they form alliances, seek synergies, and persevere. Constantly searching for ways to make a difference, they recognize that their goals are greater than themselves. Open to exploration and experimentation, their guiding principle is, "Life is what you make of it, so let's make a difference!"

I advised both CEOs to take a step back in meetings to listen and observe their teams' operating systems. I encouraged them to ask each team member to lead a meeting, which included creating the agenda and identifying the desired outcomes. The objective was for them to experience the responsibilities of leadership and engage them in exploring possibilities and solutions.

It was also crucial for Mike and Max to refrain from reinforcing victim mindsets and behaviors. By jumping in to fill the initiative gap, they had fueled the belief that only they as CEOs could frame problems, make decisions, and ask people to take action.

REDEFINING RESPONSIBILITY AND ACCOUNTABILITY

Many people have experienced work cultures where they were expected to focus on their assigned tasks, make occasional suggestions, and express disagreement indirectly. However, this approach can lead to burnout for leaders and team members, perpetuate disempowering explanations for team dysfunction, and impede efforts to improve team processes.

Outdated leadership models emphasizing top-down authority no longer serve us in today's complex and rapidly changing world. Instead, we must recognize that responsibility lies with every team member, not just those in leadership positions.

As we reset roles, it's crucial to distinguish between accountability and responsibility as we introduced in the *Foundations* chapter.

Accountability is being answerable to someone else for fulfilling what you have agreed to complete.

Accountability refers to managing the promises you make, whether they involve job functions, projects, or specific tasks within a project. The essence of accountability is being answerable to someone else—the team leader, the customer, or your peers—for fulfilling what you have agreed to complete and achieving results you have agreed to accomplish.

Responsibility involves leveraging your skills and resources to address what matters to you and others within the broader context of the team or organization. In essence, responsibility is about taking a stand for the success of the team and each other, rather than only being accountable for what you have agreed to perform yourself. Responsible team members proactively offer ideas, support, and action to address gaps and ensure success. Responsibility stems from each team member's dedication to the shared promise of the team.

Another way to understand responsibility is by examining its components: *response* and *ability*. How shall I respond to the situation in front of me, given the shared promise of our team? How can I apply my unique abilities to help the team fulfill that promise? Responsibility means choosing to apply your skills and resources to take care of the promises you have made with others.

In their excellent book, *The Power of Owning Up*, Bob Dunham and Sameer Dua explain the difference: "Responsibility is a relationship we have with ourselves about a commitment. Accountability is a relationship between two people, where one holds the other to account with judgments about the results that they produce."[53] In this way, "Responsibility entails accountability, but accountability doesn't necessarily entail responsibility."[54]

To perform well, teams need both. Without accountability, performance suffers. Without responsibility to shared promises, there is no team—just individuals accomplishing tasks in parallel.

Yes, accountability is crucial. When teams are struggling, their executives often push to improve accountability. However, inviting responsibility to a shared promise is usually a more powerful place to start.

KEEP A FORWARD-LOOKING PERSPECTIVE

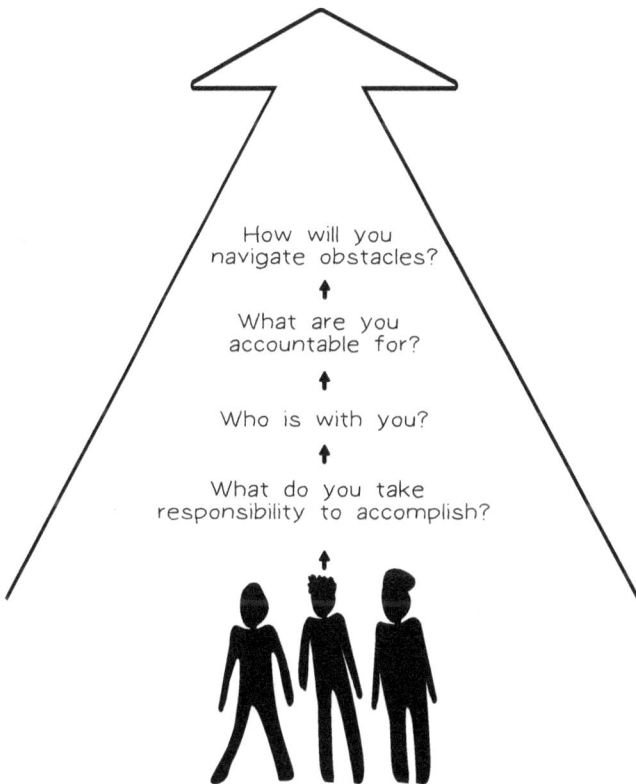

How will you
navigate obstacles?

↑

What are you
accountable for?

↑

Who is with you?

↑

What do you take
responsibility to accomplish?

↑

WHAT CAUSES A LACK OF RESPONSIBILITY?

In our experience working with teams, the most frequent cause is fear of failure: What happens if I'm all in but can't make it happen? What we see underneath this fear is low trust: Can I trust my team to help me rather than blame me? Can I trust myself and my team to work hard, learn fast, overcome obstacles, and sustain the effort?

A well-functioning team may operate quite differently from the learning environments in which many of us grew up. If we start falling behind in a team, our teammates join us in thinking through the situation, inventing solutions, pooling resources, and sustaining energy to accomplish the goal.

People also resist responsibility when they haven't been sufficiently involved. This is typically when they're handed a target and told to be accountable, instead of being invited to be responsible for a promise. They may not be familiar with the purpose—what this will accomplish for the organization and stakeholders—and how fulfilling this responsibility takes care of something about which they care personally.

There are common signs we see when team members avoid responsibility:

- Focusing solely on their tasks instead of the output of the team.
- Disengaging: avoiding team meetings and one-to-ones.
- Blaming others for mistakes and failures.
- Offering excuses for missed deadlines or performance gaps.
- Avoiding challenging tasks, projects, and conversations.
- Speaking from a perspective of self-pity.
- Avoiding initiating ways to move forward.
- Failing to raise their own performance gaps—hoping other problems on the team will prompt a reset before their individual gaps are discovered.

We can identify when responsibility is missing by paying attention to these signs. We can then go have the conversations to figure out the factors at play and invite team members to re-commit. In doing so, we promote responsibility in others and demonstrate our commitment to the team's success.

EVERYONE IS RESPONSIBLE FOR TEAM RESULTS

Herb Johnson

CEO, HVJ ASSOCIATES, INC.

Choosing to be responsible is the cornerstone of HVJ, our $40 million civil engineering business that has grown substantially over four decades.

Eight years ago, we developed and pioneered a franchise business model—the first in the country for professional engineering services. HVJ franchisee companies have been formed by trusted former employees of the firm.

With significant innovation comes leadership changes and challenges. To succeed in this franchising model, we needed to reset our promises, manage differently, and navigate new opportunities and problems as they arise. Juliana and Jan Irene of Altus helped our team grapple with responsibility for the expanded promises we asked of our executive team and of franchisees.

The study of generative leadership principles taught me, as the Founder and CEO, that I'm not integral to all decisions in a company. No one is. My job is to articulate the vision, define the game we're playing, and facilitate the forum for team members to play the game to their best ability. Everyone on our team has a role with responsibility for team results as well as accountability for specific actions.

Shared responsibility prompts us to sustain an environment of alignment and continual improvement. We muster the courage to give and receive feedback, examine our limiting beliefs, and work through issues deeply, no matter what uncomfortable feelings arise. Blame, excuses, and complaints are noticed and turned around to find our own responsibility to create the future.

Through ongoing conversation, we are achieving our vision of a high-performing, supportive, resilient team. We're proud that as we innovate and learn we continue to grow in revenue, profitability, and stakeholder satisfaction.

CULTIVATING RESPONSIBILITY IS A TEAM EFFORT

Fostering a culture of responsibility within a team is essential for success. It's frustrating for everyone when people act as victims—even if they're still performing the fundamental tasks of their roles—as this robs the team of forward-moving energy and undermines trust.

A lack of responsibility seldom corrects on its own. On the contrary, it grows and spreads as teammates feel defensive and resentful in the face of blame and avoidance.

Some leaders tell me it's easier to ignore this problem. They say, "He is who he is, and nobody is going to change him." Or, "It's not a big deal at the moment—she's doing most of her work." Some leaders seem resigned to a lower level of what's possible, while others start resenting the person and end up firing them.

Removing someone from a team is appropriate if they cannot or will not take accountability for the outputs of their role, even with sufficient training, tools, and coaching. Removal may be appropriate for team members who are accountable for their tasks but choose not to take a posture of responsibility for the team's promise. In other words, they're willing to operate as a contractor but not as a team member.

Cultivating a culture of responsibility rests with the entire team, not only those with formal leadership roles.

Rather than calling out their lack of demonstrated responsibility, we often see effective leaders and team members *call in* these people— inviting them to connect with, share, and fulfill the team's purpose.

Cultivating a culture of responsibility rests with the entire team, not only those with formal leadership roles. All members participate in creating a team environment with open and constructive communication, where mistakes are neither condemned nor buried.

Leaders and team members also build team norms that embrace mistakes as learning opportunities. When team members feel safe to make mistakes and learn from them, they are more likely to take ownership of their actions, improve, and innovate.

LEADING THE SHIFT FROM VICTIM TO RESPONSIBILITY

Max and Mike began to see the value of shifting their CEO role toward inviting a posture of responsibility. At their next team meetings, both talked with their very different teams in similar ways. They spoke directly to what they wanted for the team and what they were experiencing instead.

Max said, "In my desire to make things work, I've found myself alone on the battlefield. I'm overwhelmed and burned out, and I need each of you to step up and share responsibility for accomplishing all of our goals." He shared his vision for a high-performing team, and he invited them to take clear responsibility and accountability. He also asked the team to call him out if and when he fell back into old habits of driving the decisions and filling in the gaps.

Both CEOs experienced a sense of relief and lightness—almost like a load of bricks was taken off their backs. At the same time, their leadership team members were shocked to hear what the CEOs were feeling. Most team members became willing to share that they didn't enjoy their old way of working nor find it effective. They were ready to move forward in a different way.

TEAM PRACTICES FOR RESPONSIBILITY

Now it was time to turn good intentions into standard practice. Team members took turns leading meetings and were able to learn what leadership and membership meant. The CEOs were focused on listening to the team, asking powerful questions, and giving feedback to the meeting leaders.

Max and Mike often brought the conversation back to the team's promises to customers, investors, and employees. As leadership team members affirmed their commitment to fulfill these promises, they realized this required the behaviors of responsibility: proactively addressing cross-functional interdependencies, reaching out to help overloaded departments, and moving through challenges with creativity and support rather than blame.

We coached team members individually and collectively to make requests, offers, and responsible complaints, and to bring choices and possibilities to meetings. They practiced noting when their behaviors came from a place of no choice/victimhood and considering the full range of options available.

The process required tremendous self-awareness, courage, and practice. Team members began registering their victim behaviors and mindset, then sharing their insights with the team. For example, "I've noticed my tendency to blame others when things don't go how I want. The impact of that is that I've created distrust and resentment in others. My request is that when you see me acting in this manner, you call me out on it and remind me to speak about what I can own."

Team members learned to give each other feedback in ways that build people up rather than tear them down. Team members took this to heart. They also developed a rhythm of conversations to sustain the practices. Every week, they improved. Mike's team stopped squabbling and started helping each other. Max's team stepped out of the shadows to address cross-functional processes that could only be improved together.

At both companies, month-over-month revenue and profitability soared, and retention increased. Team members grew to make bigger commitments and fulfill them together. Choosing responsibility transformed these teams.

RECOMMENDED ACTIONS

- **Identify victim mindset and behaviors within your team.** If you feel you are paddling by yourself and unable to get your team to take the initiative and solve problems, it's very likely that you have a group of people watching you perform. They've become your audience instead of your team!

- **Interrupt the behavior immediately.** Do not reinforce it or allow it to spread. Don't get trapped in the conversation about who's right and who's wrong. Instead, ask what future they want to achieve as a team and what commitments they need to make individually and as a team to have that happen.

- **Invoke responsibility by asking questions**, such as:

  - What are you committed to accomplishing—no matter what?

  - Who is your team? In other words, who holds this promise with you?

  - What requests are you making so you can fulfill your promise?

  - What will you and your team do when it seems you've run into obstacles?

- **Keep a forward-looking perspective.** Responsibility is about our commitment to create a certain kind of future. We must allow the future to be different from the past; we can't do that when we keep looking backward. To mark this shift, make a specific time for your team to talk out loud about which lessons from the past you are letting go, and what guidelines will be useful for the future you're building now.

TRUST MAKES OR BREAKS THE TEAM

Amy Vodarek

- Do you sense the real meetings happen after the scheduled team meetings?

- Does your team talk openly about individual and shared standards?

- Are you having the conversations needed to build or repair trust?

Carolyn looked around the meeting room table, watching with concern as people smiled, closed their laptops, and pushed back their chairs. Aside from a few timeline questions, the team had easily moved through their standard agenda, finishing promptly. Carolyn pointed out that the team had yet to agree on strategic initiatives. Gavin, the COO, laughed as he commented, "We'll make a decision eventually." The team members politely wished Carolyn a good day and exited the room.

Two months before, Carolyn accepted the CEO position of a recently restructured healthcare organization with a newly merged executive leadership team. The restructuring combined several departments, shifted senior managers' reporting lines, and expanded the executive team. As an experienced CEO, she knew she had to create a cohesive executive leadership team to accomplish the challenging mandate to align culture from two previously distinct entities and improve performance.

From the start, relationships felt strained. Team members were cordial, but their engagement seemed superficial and uneven. Gavin, the COO, spoke up often and in tones that conveyed cynicism. Several members seemed disengaged from the team, and people seldom raised concerns or debated ideas.

After two months of weekly meetings, progress was limited. The executive team struggled to set a clear direction for their merged clinical and operational programs. Team members tended to focus on their own departmental agendas, human resource issues, and communications—looking to Carolyn to integrate the pieces.

SEEING WHAT'S MISSING

Given her track record of creating effective teams, Carolyn knew executives needed to think beyond narrow agendas, make decisions together, and act in a coordinated manner to drive the success of the restructured organization. They would need to become transparent with their progress, ask for partnership, and take accountability for actions and outcomes they promised.

To Carolyn these executives seemed to be missing the skills and appetite to lead together. Her ambition for creating a unified, accountable leadership team was at risk, and with it, overall outcomes and her own reputation. She knew that avoiding talking about the missing relationships and conversations would itself create further distrust, as well as delaying business results.

She moved quickly to find help. My colleague and I were brought in to work with Carolyn and her team. We began by interviewing team members to understand their experiences on the team and how they made sense of the situation. We observed team meetings and started individual executive coaching sessions with all team members.

Carolyn structured meetings with time for open discussion, recognizing understanding each other's perspectives as a foundation for building trust. The team listened to one another's updates and concerns, but with minimal discussion. Underneath the agreeable tone of the conversation, we observed behaviors that suggested moods of hesitation and resignation.

It became clear that individuals were holding onto their historical roles. Private alliances and loyalties existed alongside barely hidden annoyances with newer peers. Team members didn't openly question each other but as some people spoke they would disengage—checking emails and avoiding eye contact. Outside of team meetings, operational business was handled in small silos of mini meetings among subgroup members.

The team seemed undecided whether they would allow Carolyn to lead. Some members said yes to her requests in group settings but privately disagreed and delayed action. Frustration with Carolyn and the team also surfaced indirectly from directors and staff, who listened as executive team members vented and complained instead of resolving their disagreements.

SPEAKING ABOUT WHAT'S MISSING

We noted Carolyn had not shared her vision for the team or the organization, so her bold direction wasn't apparent to the team. She requested that team members work together to develop coordinated initiatives for the organization, but she had not asked for their explicit commitment. She hesitated to hold people accountable for slow progress or missed deadlines, which were often pushed out without discussion.

With coaching, Carolyn recognized that her patient approach needed to shift to generate results. She decided to address this head-on in the next meeting, where she catalogued with her team what was missing:

- Clearly articulated vision.
- Commitment from all executives to that vision.
- Psychological safety for team members to openly challenge, share unconventional ideas, ask for help, and raise concerns.
- Defined behaviors for success including timelines, making explicit requests, listening for sincere promises, and holding one another accountable with grace and clarity.
- Team values, standards, and agreements, including maintaining the confidentiality of the team conversations and addressing dissatisfaction directly.
- Defining and committing to a shared set of strategic initiatives, relative priorities, and the sequence of action required to implement them.
- Team recognition of Carolyn's authority to lead the organization.

Underneath it all, the team had not addressed the lack of trust among team members and between the team and Carolyn. The result was guarded communication and lack of progress. In avoiding addressing mistrust, they gave away their power as leaders to improve their situation.

FIVE DIMENSIONS OF TRUST

Trust is often discussed as either present or absent: we trust some-one, or we don't.

However, if we want to build or re-build trust, we must reflect more deeply. To start, we need to become aware of the standards already existing in our own minds for deciding the extent to which we trust someone. These standards tend to address five dimensions:[55]

To what extent do I trust their. . .

Sincerity	Care	They care about me and the future we're creating together.
	Intention	I respect what they want to accomplish.
	Motivation	I respect why they want to accomplish it.
Competence	Competence	They meet standards for effectiveness in relevant areas.
	Learning	They are rapidly growing their competence.
Reliability	Reliability	They do what they say they will.
	Capacity	They have hours in the week to allocate to this.
	Steadiness	They are consistent in their priorities and practices.
Honest	Honesty	What they say truth as they know it.
	Appropriate candor	They say what is theirs to say and no more.
	Vulnerability	They acknowledge they have things to learn.
Respect	Respect	They care how I am treated as a person.
	Listening	They pay attention to me, and I have influence with them.

For each person on a team, each other member has made assessments about the extent to which each person, including themselves, meets their own private and often unexamined standards in each of these five dimensions of trust. So, for a team of, say, seven people, that's already 245 assessments about trust—most of which have formed without thoughtful consideration!

---

*We need to become aware of
the standards already existing in
our own minds for deciding
whether we trust someone.*

Furthermore, people grant trust in specific domains—for example, you may trust a particular team member to present influentially to the board but not to develop a financial model. This mistrust could arise from a question of competence (you assess they don't know how to create financial models) or from another factor such as respect (you assess they don't listen well enough to the finance department to use their data accurately).

Additionally, these assessments are in constant motion. Each time a team member takes action, the other team members may or may not update their perception of their trustworthiness.

As we see, trust is profoundly complex and dynamic, especially in teams. Given the importance of trust to effective teaming, and the scarcity of time in most organizations, what can leaders and team members do to build or repair trust?

TRUST ISN'T SOMETHING WE HAVE, IT'S SOMETHING WE DO.

TRUST ISN'T SOMETHING WE HAVE, IT'S SOMETHING WE DO

As we've worked with hundreds of teams, including Carolyn's, we have seen them take powerful, practical steps that succeed in building trust. Each happens in conversation.

First, articulate several standards in these five dimensions of trust that are important to you and to the team's success.

For each of us, our individual, familial, cultural, academic, and organizational history shape our expectations. When people come together in teams, they bring their own perspectives on what others should do—and these perspectives often feel so obvious and valuable that they are seldom spoken. Inevitably, team members violate or appear to violate each other's unspoken standards, and mistrust emerges.

However, when team members are open about their personal standards for trusting people and their work, the team can negotiate a reasonable set of standards they can share. At their best, teams describe standards that welcome and develop individual strengths as they support high performance. We've found it helpful to start by focusing on a handful of standards that are vital to performance and/ or matter to team members as people.

For Carolyn, the dimensions of intentions, competence, and respect were critical to trust on this team. While executives seemed well-intentioned in supporting their own departments, she did not trust their commitment to the success of the new team. Carolyn held cross-functional problem-solving as a central competence for leadership team members. Finally, her standards for respect included expressing disagreement in the room, rather than in the hall later.

Second, recognize and question the assessments you've made about each other's trustworthiness in these areas.

Carolyn's team came from two distinct team experiences with different ways of working. Each group of senior leaders had built a narrative that members of the other group were not reliable. Since members started with low trust, they seldom interacted, so they had little opportunity to update their assessments of each other as unreliable. In this self-reinforcing negative cycle of isolation and mistrust, members relied on their prior relationships, undermining Carolyn's efforts to establish effective collaboration.

This reveals the most important competence for building high-trust teams: the ability to have productive conversations about these five dimensions of trust.

Pause for a moment and bring to mind a leader or team member with whom you've worked who has built teams that operate with trust. Consider, what happens on these teams that seldom happens on low-trust teams. Almost certainly, you'll see that high-trust teams can talk with each other about people's intentions, capacity, and even competence—and have these conversations in ways that invite learning, rather than blame and shame.

For example, a team member may question an aspect of another's competence: "If I remember correctly, you have little experience negotiating facilities contracts. If that's so, what can we do to make sure you bring the skill we need here?" They may discover the team member has sufficient competence to meet the standard or that additional steps or support are needed.

Since many leaders and team members have never learned to talk about dimensions of trust, these conversations can seem unfamiliar, even unimaginable. Yet, in our work with teams across levels and industries, we see that any team that wants to have these conversations well can learn to do so.

On teams that learn how to have these conversations, members can talk openly about standards, repair misunderstandings or missteps in performance, give and receive feedback, and learn from each other. These conversations also create the conditions for teams to achieve high performance, adapt to changing conditions, and grow individually and together.

Third (and sometimes first or second!), identify ways your own behaviors can become more worthy of your team members' trust.

Each of us— no matter how successful and no matter how ethical or trustworthy we see ourselves— have opportunities to interact with our teams in ways that produce deeper trust.

Begin by auditing yourself. On which of the five dimensions could I be showing up as more trustworthy and what behaviors would demonstrate this? You can ask for a coach, mentor, or trusted colleague to share their observations. As your team develops the capacity to talk constructively about these dimensions, you can gain perspectives directly.

Through feedback and our observations, Carolyn came to see that, although in many ways she was a competent as a CEO, she was not fully skilled in clearly communicating her vision for the organization and the standards for her team, and this cost her trust with the team. Because she had the courage to see this and ask for guidance, she quickly built her competence. In doing so, she role modeled openness and learning for her team.

BUILDING TRUST TO PARTNER ACROSS ORGANIZATIONAL CULTURES

Kaytura Felix, MD
DISTINGUISHED SCHOLAR, JOHNS HOPKINS
BLOOMBERG SCHOOL OF MEDICINE

In 2016, I was offered a challenging opportunity to lead a team at a large not-for-profit organization with billions of dollars in assets. The organization was undergoing a significant transformation and had launched a ten-year, $400 million strategic initiative to advance its new vision. The initiative was a collaboration of five organizations, including my own, and my role was to lead the team that guided the initiative.

Sensing the complexity of this endeavor, I brought in Amy's team. She helped me see how mistrust was emerging from the clash of different organizational cultures, and this lack of trust created tension and conflict. Our work focused on strengthening my internal team's ability to build understanding and trusting relationships within this complexity.

With Amy and Kobe's guidance, I learned how to create a safe space for team members to share their observations and opinions, and team members learned how to create safety for each other. I also learned to listen for what each individual team member wanted from me, their work, and their careers, so I could respond appropriately.

Our team's mood shifted from anxiety and resignation toward productive engagement. As we gained trust with each other, we became more optimistic and united. Our team succeeded in setting a more positive and productive tone for the larger initiative. As a result, we were able to move this massive initiative forward. Additionally, our team grew its capacity to establish strategic partnerships in other areas.

CAROLYN AND HER TEAM BUILD TRUST

Carolyn created a powerful reset by declaring the breakdown. She stated her vision and asked for clear commitment from the executive team to the vision and to their team.

We coached Carolyn and the team for the following year, both individually and during meetings. We shared insights with the team about specific patterns of behavior that contributed to the lack of trust and others that built trust. Individual coaching helped team members to identify missing conversations, turn complaints into requests, and make choices about transforming alliances into effective, full-team coordination.

Carolyn requested, and the team agreed, to have courageous conversations in the meetings or request individual discussions—rather than talking about colleagues in destructive ways. This one change became central to their progress over the first several months.

Each member grows faster under conditions of trust, and the team becomes more effective together beyond a mere sum of individuals.

Carolyn began to structure meetings more intentionally to focus on making decisions and further commitments. Before making commitments, executives addressed their teams' capacity and competency to establish reliability. Meetings included time to examine how they worked together and discuss the wins and challenges of teaming.

With coaching guidance, the team learned to share ideas and hesitations, listen fully, challenge thinking constructively, and build better reasoning together. They came to value each other's work as their own and take responsibility for their success as a team. They learned to respect each other's areas of high competence while speaking directly to the areas where peers needed to grow or gain support. The mood of the team shifted from frustration and resignation to confidence and positive ambition.

Carolyn initiated monthly individual meetings with each executive to listen for their cares and commitment to the team and develop shared understanding and priorities. She practiced listening for commitment and asking better questions to surface alternative perspectives and interpretations. Carolyn and team members developed a practice of asking open-ended and self-reflective questions, including, "What might I be missing?" The team began to make time during and between meetings to learn what each other cared about and invest in building the foundation for trust to grow.

The breakdown between Carolyn and her team led them to discover new ways to lead the organization together. They worked through historical divides and strategic misalignments, clarified their standards and processes, and developed practices to handle problems together. As a result, the unhelpful alliances dissipated, replaced by transparency, energizing conversations, accountability. The business thrived, and the leadership team became proud of their work together.

When entire teams master these conversations, we see their performance soar. Each member grows faster under conditions of trust, and the team becomes more effective together beyond a mere sum of individuals. Teams that operate with high trust unlock tremendous power to shape their future.

RECOMMENDED ACTIONS

- **Observe and listen for key dimensions of trust on your team** and note the ones that seem most important now. Building trust is an ongoing practice, as business demands change and new people enter the team.

- **Define standards for behavior with your team** and secure agreement and commitment from all members.

- **Learn and practice trust-building conversations** bringing curiosity instead of judgment. Develop competency on your team to address concerns directly, give and receive feedback, and make clear requests and promises— including asking for and offering help.

- **Be trustworthy.** Clarify and communicate your intentions. Identify areas to develop further competence and invest in your own growth. Do what you say you will do. Handle confidential conversations appropriately. Listen to your team members with genuine respect.

- **Establish a regular rhythm of team and paired conversations.** Schedule specific time with individuals and the team to check on the health of the team beyond immediate tasks and breakdowns—discuss coordination, alignment, and progress against team standards, strategic priorities, and the organization's vision.

RELATIONSHIPS DRIVE TEAM PERFORMANCE

Sailaja Manacha

- Which relational needs matter in the workplace?
- How do these needs show up on teams and impact performance?
- How can leaders best address the relational needs of their teams?

Jason, a leader in a large multinational technology firm, told me of the deep mutual respect he has for his boss. The company wished to entrust Jason with a new role and geographic territory. His boss knew the move would serve the company well, but would not be in Jason's best interests. The boss intervened with the board to protect Jason from the new "opportunity" and set up a more promising path.

Jason reminisced about how he felt strongly supported when his leader stepped up to advocate on his behalf and how protected he felt vis-à-vis his career and aspirations. His boss had his back, and that meant a lot to Jason.

This sense of connection and gratitude arises when a leader understands their team members and aims to address individual needs. Meeting relational needs is a crucial component of employee engagement. A Gallup study shows that companies in the top quartile for employee engagement outperform their competitors in the lowest quartile in many categories, including 21% higher profitability and 41% lower absenteeism.[56] As an executive coach and psychotherapist, I frequently see a direct relationship between a leader's understanding of the relational needs of their team and how effectively that team performs.

WHY DO RELATIONAL NEEDS MATTER AT WORK?

Relational needs are the central human desires that can be met only through social interaction, including family, work, and friendships. These needs are present in all stages of our life from birth to death, and each of us has our own unique ordering of the needs that matter most. We may not be aware of them, but if they're not met, we experience a deep inner longing. In any kind of crisis, they're likely to come to the surface.

Since we bring our whole selves to work each day, we bring these longings within us as well. Psychotherapist Richard Erskine describes relational needs as an essential aspect of the universal human desire for connection.[57] We may not be consciously aware of them, but we still hope these needs can be fulfilled at work, given the multitude of relationships we share and the many hours we spend working.

When I coach clients who are experiencing a health crisis or professional burnout, I often find an unaddressed relational need lurking in the background. Their inner chatter may sound like "There's nobody there for me," "You're always on your own," "It's lonely at the top—no one understands," or "Nobody can be trusted."

In today's workplace, conversational time is scarce; the focus is on taking action. The fast pace and high ambiguity often leave people feeling like they're on a treadmill, gasping for breath. It's hard to prioritize connection and conversation, although cognitively we may understand these are foundational to trust, collaboration, and productivity.

> *Teams require a commitment to creating a future together. When individuals don't feel seen, understood, or valued, they seldom commit fully.*

When relational needs are not met, they become more intense, more pressing, and more immediate. Some people may become frustrated, angry, or aggressive in the face of unmet needs. Others become depressed, lose energy, and burn out. This shows up at work as disconnected groups of individuals, rather than teams.

Teams require a commitment to creating a future together. When individuals don't feel seen, understood, or valued, they seldom commit fully.

Consider these questions:

- When was the last time you felt truly enthusiastic at work? Were you energized by just the goal you were working towards or also the camaraderie with other people?

- When you last worked with a leader with whom you could discuss almost anything, what conversations and experiences helped you build trust?

- Think about when you last worked on a stretch goal. Was it the incentive that motivated you, or, at least in part, your relationship with the leader and team that had you wanting to give your best?

When I ask these questions, the responses almost always include elements of relational aspects between the leader and team member, as well as relationships with peers. Gallup has found that managers' attitudes and involvement account for 70% of the variance in employee engagement scores within an organization.[58] We're wired to respond to relationship and connection, as these are deep human needs.

We need to feel safe in order to be ourselves.

Being aware of these needs in ourselves and in others can help us grow and strengthen human relationships. This awareness can also help us gain insight into and empathy for the feelings, behaviors, and motivations of ourselves and others. We're more likely to respond to our teammates in ways that build connection and trust.

SIX RELATIONAL NEEDS THAT SHOW UP ON TEAMS

As a team leader, your competence to produce effective teamwork depends in part on your ability to see and address these six relational needs.

The Need for Security

We need to feel safe in order to be ourselves, without fear of being shamed, blamed, or discounted for what we say or who we are. We need acceptance of the thoughts and feelings we share with others without fear of being judged.

Amy Edmondson, leadership professor at Harvard Business School, refers to psychological safety, quoting a study of what differentiated average teams from excellent ones at Google.[59] She states that feeling comfortable enough to speak up and express oneself is a key factor in establishing team excellence. In such a team, members feel confident no one on the team will embarrass or punish anyone else for admitting a mistake or asking a question.[60]

Within teams, we often claim that we listen with openness and respect all views. However, we need to go beyond words. Trust is a somatic "felt" experience that what we offer is being treated with respect: We feel it in our bodies.[61] For example, we may be sharing a vulnerability (such as a lack of experience with part of our job) or a sensitive aspect of our life. When we don't experience a sense of safety, we withhold information, insights that could improve performance, and unique perspectives that could give our team the benefits of diversity.

Our needs also include physical safety. A young member of a team spoke of how her manager always showed concern when she worked late. The manager arranged for her safe travel and checked that all was well when she arrived home at odd hours. She expressed how much she respected her leader for this care he extended towards her.

REFLECTIONS:

- How do I encourage team members to speak up—especially if what they're expressing is different from the prevailing view?

- If I have a colleague whose views are different from others on the team, or one who dresses differently, or has different life pursuits—how do I convey they are a valued part of the team?

- When people seem frustrated, how do I convey to them that I've heard and respect their concerns?

The Need to be Affirmed as Significant

This is the need to be appreciated and respected not only for what we do but also for who we are.

Vini is a leader in a large multinational. She told me that in her current role, she feels like she is shriveling: "What I do doesn't matter. I don't matter." She feels senior management isn't taking her seriously and isn't offering opportunities for which she is asking—despite having proved her competence over a dozen years of highly rated work. Vini said, "They don't think I am important enough to keep me informed. I feel a loss of dignity as I keep following up." I could hear the deep disappointment in her voice.

We have all at some time or another experienced the joy of being acknowledged for our value and significance. As a coaching client put it, "Working with this leader makes my spine stronger, and I feel taller by an inch." We typically experience such validation when we're understood by others. What a difference it makes when our team leader makes time to listen to the bits of our personal histories that we choose to share, our thoughts about our current capabilities and the results we are creating, our experiences on the team, and how we may wish to grow in our roles and throughout our careers.

REFLECTIONS:

- How often do I look each team member in the eye and make time to listen with my full presence?

- How do I coach members to bring the best of their unique capabilities in ways that strengthen the team, rather than rewarding conformity?

- How often do I affirm people and recognize their contributions so that team members' skills and strengths are seen by others?

The Need for Protection and Opportunity from a Dependable Person

As children, we look up to and rely on parents, teachers, and elders for their protection, information, and encouragement. This dynamic is also present in organizational life and built into the hierarchy of a manager and subordinate relationship—whether we want this or not.

Lisa, one of my clients, wanted to expand her contributions to the company, but wasn't seeing interest from her boss. Finally, she asked for a meeting with her boss's boss and conveyed her hopes and concerns. She was disappointed that this leader made no attempt to learn about her abilities or listen to how she might be able to contribute more. She decided to leave—prompted as much by a need to feel seen and valued as by the desire for a larger role.

As many of us have heard, people leave managers rather than companies.[62] We look to leaders to be stable and dependable people who will give us helpful information, guide our growth, and protect our interests. While capable teams can meet much of this need for stability and support, we want to know that we can also count on the official leaders of our tribe.

REFLECTIONS:

- When a team member is overwhelmed, how often do I connect with them so they know they are supported?

- When a team member has messed up, how have I given constructive feedback while communicating that I have their back?

- How do I create opportunities for team members, so they're deepening their strengths and growing in their careers?

We need to define ourselves as unique and to have others accept and respect that uniqueness.

The Need for Self-Definition

We need to define ourselves as unique and to have others accept and respect that uniqueness. We want to see the special value that we bring to a task, to the team, and to the world.

Aruna led the Learning and Development team in a growing software and media technology company. When she came into the role, she realized that the organization's approach to training and learning was skill-based and transactional, while her own approach was grounded in human development. She decided to take a risk and began implementing programs that reflected her deep-dive and personal approach.

Initially, this was welcomed, and people raved about how valuable the courses were. Aruna's boss, however, was distinctly uncomfortable with her approach and began pushing her to follow more traditional skill-based methods. Aruna said, "I felt stunted—I had no permission to do this my way, even though it was yielding great results." She decided to leave the organization, as she felt her "brand" of work would not gain acceptance and support.

Her next organization welcomed her unique approach. She found the CEO and Human Resources head were curious to know more. They expressed appreciation for her efforts and gave Aruna an open canvas to design interventions that leverage her strengths.

REFLECTIONS:

- How often do I articulate to team members their unique contributions to the team, what I'm learning from them, or how what they do inspires me?

- When team members set out to accomplish results in ways that are different from mine, how often do I respond with curiosity and support?

- How often do I celebrate team members in ways that are meaningful to them and honor their distinct contributions?

The Need to Make a Positive Impact on Other People

As humans, we want to affect others in some way. Maybe we change their way of thinking, convince them to alter their behavior, or get them laughing. We also want our influence to be acknowledged by those we impact.

We need to influence others and contribute in a significant way to the results of the team.

In a work setting, we need to influence others and contribute in a significant way to the results of the team. Team members also want their contributions acknowledged by the leader and their team, adjacent teams, and customers.

For example, Harsha shared with me how disappointed she was not to have received a promotion in three years. A leader who had recently joined the team told Harsha that her competence was not on par with the demands of the new, higher role she wanted. A few days later, the leader called Harsha in for a meeting and offered to create a plan for her professional development. He committed to opening doors for her inside the organization, setting up opportunities to perform, and giving her feedback. Over a period of a year, Harsha grew tremendously, and she felt ready to move forward with a new set of competencies. "The promotion was only one growth path. Now I've grown in the real sense of the word, as I've grown my competence." I could hear in her voice the deep gratitude and regard for her leader's candid and helpful approach. As she grew, she was delighted to accomplish even more for the team and be recognized for these contributions.

REFLECTIONS:

- In a situation where a new idea or perspective is brought to the table, how do I express to team members the impact their thinking has had on me?

- In what ways do I impact others with my listening, my presence, or my challenges to them? How do I know when I have done this well?

- How often have I played a valuable role in shaping a team member's career direction? How often do I make time to learn about their career and life aspirations?

CREATING A TEAM WHERE MEMBERS FEEL HEARD AND VALUED

Dr. Rohini Srivathsa,
NATIONAL TECHNOLOGY OFFICER, MICROSOFT INDIA

Reflecting on my leadership journey, the most valuable quality I bring is building relationships within which people thrive. I've come to appreciate that trust deeply felt in the heart—not articulated or intellectualized in the head—is indeed the key ingredient of a high-functioning team.

In 2011, I had the opportunity to lead a team of senior strategy consultants at a multinational technology and business services company. The team was made up of seasoned professionals, but many were new to the organization. Over the course of three quarters, this team reinvented itself, transforming from underperforming to the top-performing team globally. The key factor was trust cultivated through transparency, consistency, humility, empathy, and a shared sense of purpose.

The team didn't need me to bring technical guidance. Instead, my role was to create an environment where team members felt heard, acknowledged, and valued, as Sailaja describes in this chapter. I helped bring the team together by establishing a shared purpose and then upheld transparency and consistency in our day-to-day functioning.

My growth as a technology executive and thought leader continues through meditation, mindfulness, coaching, and reflection. I see that the leadership qualities that emerge from inner growth and authentic relationships are increasingly important to business success.

We each have a need to have others reach out and initiate contact with us.

THE NEED TO HAVE ANOTHER PERSON CARE ABOUT US

We each have a need to have others reach out and initiate contact with us. Any relationship where one party always must take the first step to approach the other will eventually become dissatisfying.

When team members are not coordinating well or they're burying themselves in a silo of individual tasks, I recommend each member reach out to arrange more 1:1 and small group conversations. This helps them coordinate tasks and build the social bonds that facilitate conversations for professional development, process improvement, and innovation.

We also have a human need to express care towards others and to have this care accepted and valued by others. When they appreciate what we offer, we, in turn, feel valued in the relationship. When what we offer is routinely unnoticed, declined, or not valued, we feel un-appreciated and slowly back off emotionally from that relationship. Brief personal check-ins at weekly team meetings—where members can share whatever they want the team to know about their non-work lives or how they're feeling in and out of work—provide a forum for colleagues to learn about each other, express care, and offer support.

REFLECTIONS:

- How often do I reach out to team members informally, just to strengthen our connection?

- Do I ask about a team member's family and express my concern for their health and that of their family?

- How do I express affection and care to my team?

REHUMANIZING WORK

Valuing and meeting appropriate relational needs provide an oppor-tunity to rehumanize the workplace. When leaders can account for the relational needs of their team members, they set the team on course for positive outcomes.

Leading teams is a privilege—the privilege of walking the journey with others, of being a person of influence and inspiration in the life of another. Through our work, we can create safe and encouraging spaces for ourselves and others to grow. Building a team with healthy relationships—a team where we feel secure, valued, accepted, unique, influential, and connected—lets us show up to our organizations and our lives ready to engage, grow, and co-create.

RECOMMENDED ACTIONS

- **Notice the feelings and moods of your teams, and attend to relationships.**
  When the mood on your team seems tense or disengaged, check in with your team members as people. Ask how it feels to be on the team and what would help make it feel inclusive and energizing. Also, look to build committed teams and trustworthy relationships with your peers and your boss.

- **Inventory and upgrade your practices to support these six relational needs.**
  Use the questions in each section to audit your leadership practices, then take action. You can also invite feedback about what you do that supports positive, trusting relationships on the team, and what you might do differently.

- **Become aware of your own relational needs and find healthy ways to meet them.**
  Many leaders let work and personal friendships dissolve as they rise in companies. Yet, we each have needs to be valued as people, as well as performers. Identify and cultivate the relationships that bring you dignity and joy.

FINDING TEAM PROMISES IN THE BODY

Sheeja Shaju

- Have you ever sensed that your team members lack confidence in the team's goals?

- Have you noticed team members misaligned about what is to be delivered and when?

- What—in your body or their bodies—prompted you to feel this way?

Sonia sat at her desk, feeling utterly drained. She had just emerged from a business review meeting with her new team. Sonia's team included nine experienced department heads—each with impressive technical knowledge in their area of expertise. These capable leaders had spent the morning blaming each other for the lack of progress in fulfilling orders.

Sonia decided to stop the meeting to clear her head and allow others to do the same. She contacted my colleague and me after this meeting, and we set up conversations with her team to explore the situation.

Team members told us about their initial excitement last quarter when the sales head announced a massive manufacturing order. The team congratulated themselves for building the brand's reputation for quality, which was crucial to securing this order. This new order was significantly larger than typical, and they had little time to ramp up their teams to meet the delivery schedule. Work began at full speed.

However, problems soon appeared, and tempers ran short. Accustomed to working in functional silos, their teams did not coordinate sufficiently to adapt to the specifications of the new order. Early manufacturing runs produced output below quality standards.

Heads of sales, design, engineering, manufacturing, quality, and account service each thought the other teams had let them down. As the leaders' frustration and mistrust of each other snowballed throughout the company, people in their departments avoided cross-functional meetings. Communication dwindled to email exchanges, leading to frequent misunderstandings and unresolved issues.

HE SAID "YES"

Neeraj, the Quality Department head, calculated that his team needed to expand from five to nine people in the next ten days to address the increasing number of units failing standards and enable improvement processes. He rushed into the office of Sanjay, the Human Resources head and provided the position requirements. Sanjay appeared skeptical but agreed to fill and onboard these four positions in the required timeframe. As soon as Neeraj heard a "Yes," he stood up, expressed his eagerness for these new team members, and left to take care of other tasks.

Ten days passed without any interviews scheduled. Neeraj received only five resumes from HR, none of which met his standards. He felt the muscles in his neck tightening, as he realized he wouldn't be able to hire in time to fulfill the order.

For a promise to exist, there must be two parties: the one who makes the promise and the one who receives it.

LISTENING FOR THE PROMISE

For a promise to exist, there must be two parties: the one who makes the promise and the one who receives it. It's crucial that both parties take responsibility to ensure, first, that a promise is made, and second, that they hold the same definition of what was promised. We call this "listening for the promise."

Even when everyone involved believes a promise was made, often there are as many descriptions of that promise as people on the team. Meetings frequently proceed as if there was clarity, instead of pausing to check that everyone shares the same understanding of the deliverable. When work begins under these conditions, the team invests energy, time, and money aiming to fulfill their understanding of the request. Despite these efforts, their work may be deemed unsatisfactory, and they may be judged as failing to meet what was needed.

The business costs of misaligned promises are high—missed targets, unfulfilled orders, and disappointed clients.

The team costs are also high—blame, mistrust, and disengagement. Team members may withhold collaboration or micromanage each other's work. Meetings may be avoided or prolonged fruitlessly. This disengagement makes team members even less likely to communicate enough to coordinate well, further confirming their low perceptions of each other.

When Neeraj asked Sanjay to hire the four additional positions in the next ten days, this produced a misaligned promise. Neeraj made the request and felt relieved that help was on the way, while Sanjay felt confused and frustrated by this unusual and difficult request. Neeraj then moved on to other aspects of preparing for this massive order and was so busy he paid little attention to email, while Sanjay interpreted Neeraj's lack of email replies as an indication that filling the positions wasn't a priority.

Neeraj failed to gain a promise from Sanjay to produce new hires in record time. Sanjay failed to gain a promise from Neeraj to coordinate as needed as the hiring manager to ensure success. Instead of generating four new hires to take care of product quality, their conversation produced waste, frustration, and mistrust.

A WAY FORWARD: THE BODY

Look at the body language of the individuals engaged in any conversation. The body signals the emotion the individual is currently feeling. The tiniest signs are important to catch since these may help us deepen our understanding of what's brewing inside.

When we make a request of someone, we need to listen to their whole body. Many times, when we hear words like "yes" or "will do," we notice aspects of their face or posture or voice that suggest "can't do" or "won't do" would be a more appropriate answer.

We also gain insight from our own bodies. We may get a sense that the person making the promise isn't fully committed. This feeling arises within our own bodies. We might notice a tightness in the tummy, a hollow feeling in the chest, or a discomfort in the throat.

These sensations are valuable indicators—alerting us that something here doesn't line up, and it would be wise to seek further clarification. Yet, we often ignore these observations and physical cues. We act as if we heard genuine commitment to a promise.

Richard Strozzi-Heckler, renowned innovator in embodied leadership, writes in his book *The Leadership Dojo*, "In the beginning is the body. We are all born into a body, and through the body we come to know the world and ourselves. He goes on to say, "It is only through the body that we are present and make sense to others and become evident to others, the environment, and the world. This is so obvious that it's invisible to us." [63]

As we grow up, we tend to focus on how we appear outwardly to others, as well as how we ought to act in a social situation. Over time, this creates a division between what we feel within and what we show outwardly. We learn to suppress what we're feeling within us. Our bodies are constantly talking to us—but over time, we've unconsciously conditioned ourselves to ignore what they're saying.

Many of us have not practiced listening to our bodies, especially at work. Once we do, we might notice the tension in our shoulders, the fatigue in our backs, and the pit in our stomachs when we're asked to produce results that seem vague or impossible. Body awareness can motivate us to talk with our colleagues and see if together we can define promises that make sense. This opens the possibility for our bodies to feel more ease and more energy, which contributes to a more connected and productive team climate.

We've also learned to ignore what our body tells us about the body language of others—including the team member who is—or isn't—making a promise. As team interactions increasingly shift to online and asynchronous channels, we lose the context of hearing each other's voices, seeing their eyes, and experiencing their posture and body language. We fall out of practice in reading non-verbal cues.

PRACTICE OBSERVING

Bodies and voices, for example...

Decline   Decline   Accept

THE PRACTICE

In our workshops at The Institute for Generative Leadership, we invite participants to engage in a listening exercise. We pair people up and have each person says the words, "I will" to their partner. Each person is asked to say these same simple words with ten different meanings. The person might say "I will," yet mean "I might," or "I can't wait to do it!" or even, "I'm scared that I don't know how to get it done."

Listeners are asked to pay close attention to the speaker's voice, breath, and body language—observing subtle cues such as twitches, rigidness, sternness, softness, movement, energy, hesitancy, and joy. These listeners, mostly leaders in their organizations, find paying

These conversations can take time. Yet, we find misunderstandings and unspoken concerns take even longer!

attention in this way helps gauge their expectations of the speaker and, if necessary, to seek clarification to define a mutually agreeable promise. This brief activity motivates many leaders to practice listening to their teams in a deeper way.

Through this practice, we see that words can have a range of meanings, expressed more fully through voice, expression, and movement. We learn that the body reveals thoughts and emotions. When we listen to these signals on our teams, we can invite people to speak about their full range of hopes and concerns. These conversations can take time. Yet, we find misunderstandings and unspoken concerns take even longer!

Now let's come back to Neeraj and the head of Human Resources.

BUT . . . HE SAID "YES"

In the next meeting of department heads, Neeraj harshly shared how disappointed he was that HR didn't come through with the needed staff. Feeling attacked, Sanjay responded that since Neeraj didn't respond to his emails, he figured this request was no longer a priority.

During my next coaching conversation with Neeraj, we explored the situation:

- Neeraj had not been able to add new members to his team.

- Because of this, his deadlines would probably be missed, and the order might be delayed.

- Neeraj was frustrated and looking for someone to blame.

Our conversation unfolded in this way:

> **My question:** *Did the HR Head understand your conditions of satisfaction?*
>
> **Neeraj 's response:** *My conditions were very clear. Whether Sanjay understood what I meant, I'm not sure.*
>
> **Question:** *When he agreed to deliver your requests, was he sure?*
>
> **Response:** *Now to think of it, he did seem a little skeptical.*
>
> **Question:** *What made you feel he was skeptical?*
>
> **Response:** *Well, Sanjay put his hands in his pockets, furrowed his eyebrows, and said, "Hmmm," as if he was in deep thought. Then he said, "Yes" in a low tone.*

What made Neeraj sense Sanjay's skepticism? His assessment of voice and body language.

Neeraj realized that during the meeting, he had overlooked these crucial body cues. In fact, he was aiming to avoid listening to any cues from Sanjay. Had Neeraj paid closer attention and addressed them, they might have come to a shared view of the promise and hired the people they needed.

When asked to reflect on the sensations he felt in his body at the time the promise was made, Neeraj closed his eyes and paused to think. He said, "I'm not sure if I felt anything in the body, but I can honestly say one thing: I felt the urge to get out of that meeting immediately, so I wouldn't give him a chance to decline or negotiate the promise."

This confession was no surprise to me, and it's a frequent scenario in many organizations. Deep within, many leaders and team members who are hearing promises are aware that the person making the promise does not genuinely understand it or commit to delivering it. They know it's highly uncertain that the promise will be kept, yet they press forward anyway.

LEADERS LEARN TO READ THE ROOM

Tapan Singhel
MANAGING DIRECTOR AND CEO, BAJAJ ALLIANZ GENERAL INSURANCE CO. LTD.

Leaders have to keep mobilizing their teams and effectively communicate—both verbally and non-verbally. This is of paramount importance, and one cannot overinvest in this skill. The best part is that you can learn and cultivate this habit through practice.

Being a leader is also about reading a room, picking up on the elusive emotions of your clients or listeners, and basing your solutions upon them, so as to achieve collective growth. Sheeja is an exceptional program leader who helps you understand both the bold and subtle hints revealed by the human body in team interactions. I strongly believe in what she advocates, and I'm glad to see she's imparted this art here.

PRACTICING LISTENING TO BODY LANGUAGE

When we started working with Neeraj, Sanjay, and the other members of Sonia's team, we introduced them to the power of noticing bodies as we request, receive, and make promises.

At first, we asked them to become aware of and write down their own internal sensations as they move through their usual meetings. Over time, they learned to interpret these sensations and to observe themselves and others with curiosity rather than blame or shame.

Amar, the Head of Operations in Sonia's organization, decided to enter the team's daily meeting with the goal of practicing listening to body language. The team was working under a tight deadline. Sunit, one of Amar's star performers, was usually articulate about his thoughts and readily asked questions for clarity. But on this day, he was unusually quiet.

As Amar asked for a commitment to meet the deadline, Sunit remained mostly quiet. He neither expressed commitment nor said it was impossible. Instead, Sunit simply echoed what Amar said.

At the end of the meeting, Amar realized he faced two options:

- He could allow this incident to pass, since Sunit verbally agreed to the deadline.

- He could pay attention to Sunit's body language and try to understand what he wasn't able to express verbally.

Later, Amar reflected on his experience.

"A few weeks ago, I would probably have jumped at the first option. But I've since learned that it would have been a mistake to let Sunit leave without a conversation. I found him after the meeting and mentioned that I noticed he wasn't his usual self. I asked if there was something I needed to know to support him and the team. Sunit looked up and assured me everything was fine.

"However, I could sense from the way he was holding his body that there was more to it. So, I asked him again and assured him I only wanted to help him achieve the team's objective. That's when he actually opened up and said there was a personal issue distracting him. After speaking a bit more, we agreed that he could take the rest of the day off to take care of what he had to do so that he could be fully present for what needed to be done at work. I felt satisfied with that decision, and I could see the relief on Sunit's face."

When you hear a promise, pay attention to your own body as well.

Often, people shy away from addressing non-verbal cues, fearing a conversation might be intrusive. Yet, if you care about the outcome, the team member's reputation, and the team's culture, then it's critical to connect and aim to understand more deeply.

Make a practice of observing bodies, voice, and language when people accept or decline requests. The more you practice, the more skillful you will become at noting incongruencies that are worth investigating. When you hear a promise, pay attention to your own body as well. Can you discern the difference between a trustworthy promise and one that leaves you feeling uncertain? The more aware you are of these signs, the more choices you'll have in responding to these situations.

WHAT HAPPENS WHEN TEAMS PAY ATTENTION TO PROMISES

Over the next eight months, we worked closely with Sonia and each department head, coaching them on new ways of working with their teams. We focused on listening to promises from bodies and voices, clarifying what was meant by a promise, and communicating openly. The team also learned to take the risk to follow up when they were unclear about a team member's commitment to a promise, and to do so effectively.

The changes started with department heads making and seeking trustworthy promises. Most promises were now either met or renegotiated to ensure fulfillment. Finger-pointing faded, and the leadership team grew more collaborative, knowing they could trust each other to deliver.

The leaders then started working with their departmental teams and inviting them to participate in candid, productive conversations about their promises. Over time, Sonia noticed a more positive culture throughout the organization, and clients noticed an increase in product quality and more reliable delivery.

When team members listen for promises and how promises live in bodies, they create a more reflective space where they can shape the future together.

RECOMMENDED ACTIONS

- **Listen for promises.** In meetings this week, jot down every promise you think you may have heard. How clear are these promises? Do all parties share a common view of what is to be delivered? Does the promise seem trustworthy, or does it feel uncertain or conflicted?

- **Pay attention to your body.** Recognize the sensations within your own body when making or receiving a promise. Keep a journal of the promises you've made and note what you feel in your body about each of these. Given the information from your body, what next action might you take so that you and the team can manage these promises effectively?

- **Observe others with genuine curiosity.** If a team member's voice is unusually curt or their posture is disengaged, that may or may not have much to do with the topic being discussed. Yet, while they're in this state, it may be hard for them to express a trustworthy promise. If the promise matters, you may want to explore this one-to-one.

- **Invite your team to real-time conversations.** Promises made in email or apps always contain the seeds of misalignment. For important matters, aim to talk by voice, video, or in person.

- **Welcome open dialogue.** Create a safe environment where team members feel comfortable discussing their concerns, seeking clarification, and offering support.

BUILDING TEAMS IN A COMPLEX AND DIVERSE WORLD

CREATING DIVERSE AND BRAVE TEAMS

Steven E. Jones, PhD

- What diversity, including racial differences, shows up in your team?

- Who is present but without an equal voice? Who is missing?

- How do you tap into the power and energy of diverse voices?

Many of us envision ways life could be better for ourselves, our neighbors, or our co-workers. We might be willing to take action, but there's no way to make it happen ourselves. What we need is a team—a diverse team that understands and engages the entire community or organization to create a better future.

Let's follow the journey of Dana, a physician concerned about the ten-year disparity in life expectancy across racial groups in his city and what could be done to close the gap. From a 25-year career dedicated to treating patients and promoting public health, Dana knew that improving life span for marginalized people would increase their well-being and create positive effects across the city.

As in many communities, there was a profound disparity in the life expectancy of prosperous Whites, compared to Blacks, Asians, and Latinos across all economic groups. Factors compromising life expectancy include undertreated medical conditions, working conditions, stress, and environmental factors rooted in systemic biases. Dana's initial conversations with local leaders revealed they were unfamiliar with the reality of health inequities and tended to doubt that people of color were living shortened lives in their beloved city.

Dana discussed the discrepancy with the staff of epidemiologists and medical professionals, who were skilled at using data to make decisions. They confirmed the data showed substantial and persistent differences in life expectancy between Black and White community members. With Dana's leadership, the public health staff decided to tackle the challenge of eradicating racial life span disparity in their city.

FORMING A BROAD, DIVERSE, AND COMMITTED TEAM

Given the size and difficulty of their goal, these public health professionals chose to become a team committed both to this big promise and to supporting each other throughout the journey. They formed a core team of people drawn from the city public health department, and added two community leaders with high credibility and experience in bringing people together.

This core team was knowledgeable and capable, yet they knew their best efforts would be insufficient to tackle a problem this large. To generate meaningful and lasting results, the initiative needed systemic strategies that touched many parts of community life. They asked me to partner with them to build a broader external change team to guide citywide action. By joining with others beyond their public health staff, they could gain community support, design relevant solutions, engage people with varied skills, and create change.

Members of both teams would need to commit to the same promise: to improve life expectancy and well-being for all the city's residents, especially people of color. If successful, they knew they would improve lives for generations to come.

Teams and communities can develop their capability for antiracist understanding and action.

The core team identified potential change team members very thoughtfully. They needed people invested in the city's success with strategic skills, organizational support, a track record of follow-through, and commitment to improving the lives of marginalized people.

Dana knew the change team also needed to mirror the diversity of the city. Diversity comes in many forms: race, gender identity, education, economic class, faith, age, and others. At Altus, we see value from diversity when people from differing backgrounds and experiences come together to build spaces where each person knows that they belong and where they live and work in an equitable environment that helps them to thrive.

Race is often the most challenging form of diversity to address in building teams. This arises for many reasons, including racially limited personal networks, biases about who can contribute effectively, and inexperience in discussing one's own racial identities and those of others. Teams and communities can develop their capability for antiracist understanding and action by engaging a critical mass of non-Black members to learn about the lived experience of people of other races, identify systematic barriers to equity, and honor differences through effective conversations.[64]

The core team pushed themselves to think broadly about community needs and reach outside their own personal networks. Based on thoughtful analysis, they invited racially diverse leaders from businesses, hospitals, fire and police departments, government agencies, educational institutions, libraries, faith groups, and non-governmental organizations. The invitees held essential knowledge of the community and, critically, authority to take action in their respective domains.

Each of us views the world differently based on our own personal history and choices.

Before invitees joined the change team, Dana and the core team asked what was important to them—personally, and as representatives of their institution. Dana, the core team, and change team invitees sat down to explore how joining forces would help them take care of what they wanted to accomplish in the city. These conversations about shared purpose produced crucial alignment for navigating diverse perspectives on how to accomplish the promise.

MAKING THE MOST OF OUR DIFFERENCES

Research shows that once understanding and trust are built, more diverse teams develop better solutions than teams who observe the world similarly.[65] Lack of diversity across decisionmakers is in part how we wind up with racial health disparities. Dana was determined not only to select members with varied backgrounds, networks, skills, and perspectives, but to ensure those members were fully included.

Applying the **OAAR model**—Observer, Actor, Action, Results— helped the change team gain the benefits of their diversity.[66]

The **Observer** recognizes that each of us views the world differently based on our own personal history and choices. No two people in any room perceive the same things in the same way. The power of diversity in teams comes from different observers who share their perspectives. This enables the entire team to think more comprehensively.

THE POWER OF DIVERSITY IN TEAMS

Comes from different observers
who share their perspectives.

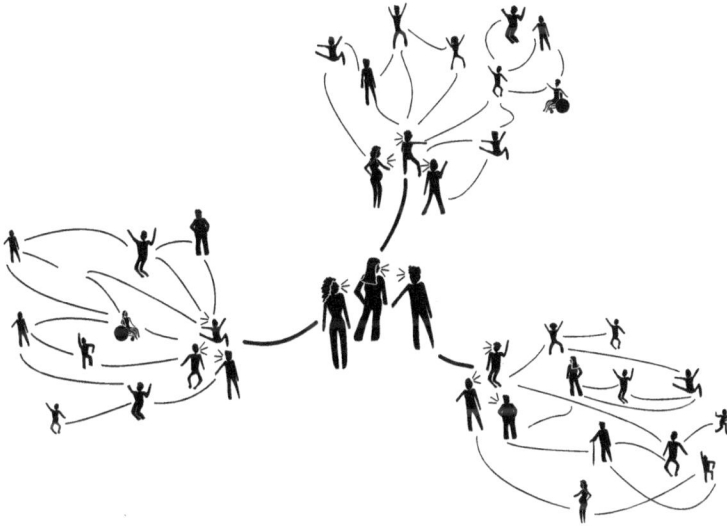

People are also different **Actors:** We have varied ways of gathering input, making decisions, and coordinating with others.

Actions and **Results** spring from people who see their world and want to create a better future. We create teams because we want results. Yet, when teams are built in a rush for action and results, the value of each person as an observer and actor is often missed, and results falter. Teams with diverse members can tap the benefits of diversity only when they respect and learn from team members' unique observations and capabilities for action.

Dana understood that accomplishing the ambitious aim of closing the life expectancy gap depended on inviting and hearing the diverse perspectives of team members.

TAKING CARE OF WHAT WE CARE ABOUT

Teams are built through conversations. The core and change teams often started meetings by connecting to what they cared about: the well-being of all community members. In our approach to leadership, where we equip people to generate new outcomes, *care* is the foundation of all actions and commitments, as described in Bob Dunham's sidebar in the *Foundations* chapter. Care is "the source of the energy and meaningfulness of our commitments. Throughout our lives, care lives in our bodies. In the stories we tell, it connects us to our commitments and actions."[67] In this case, the teams' shared care was long, healthy lives for everyone in the community.

A powerful shift occurs when people who share their care commit to creating a new future work together. Where there used to be people wishing, ignoring, attempting, or even complaining, now there's a team taking purposeful action.

The change team met monthly—a cadence that allowed people to learn, deepen relationships, and test initial insights from what they observed in the community. They started by looking at data regarding *Social Determinants of Health*—conditions in the places where people live, learn, and work that affect a wide range of health risks and outcomes. The city's data made clear the discrepancies between social determinants of health for different racial groups correlated with and contributed to differences in life expectancy.

Their discoveries matched what we know: racial disparities create adverse effects that compound over the lifetime of children, women, and men. Systematic oppression and racism bring health consequences, including higher rates of diabetes, high blood pressure, heart disease, cancer, asthma, and other illnesses. Parallel factors, such as safety and economic disparities, also shorten life spans. Marginalized communities often lack the political influence to enforce environmental regulations, provide safe childcare and eldercare, and even install streetlights. Families facing structural poverty lack the resources to mitigate health risks on their own. As the team presented the data on life expectancy inequity, they raised awareness and opened new choices for city leaders to promote the health of Black people and other marginalized residents.

WORKING WITH UNCOMFORTABLE EMOTIONS

The core team needed to open and guide conversations about systematic racism, implicit biases, White privilege, and racial injustice—with the change team first, then through them to the entire community. They knew this wouldn't be easy, and it wasn't. Talking about bias and race tends to bring up emotional reactions that many people are unaccustomed to working through constructively.

When working with teams, we pay attention to the emotions that show up, since emotions either open possibilities or close them.[68] When discussing race, feelings such as anger, fear, guilt, and shame often emerge. Team members' discomfort around these emotions in themselves or others can impel them to withdraw or act unskillfully, which closes possibilities. When people are willing to be uncomfortable for the sake of a bigger promise, possibilities open.

As leaders and team members, we are responsible for noticing the emotional state of our colleagues. We can pay attention when people are experiencing fear, confusion, excitement, or anger. By responding skillfully to these emotions in ourselves and others, we can expand the emotions that power the work and allow less helpful emotions to diminish. By fostering emotions that mobilize human capacity to pursue a goal, we fortify our teams for the work ahead. Inviting moods of curiosity, camaraderie, and determination strengthens us. We can see more, hear others more fully, decide wisely, and act bravely.

Building the mind and body to handle unfamiliar conversations means teams can address the most difficult problems in their world.

Emotions live in bodies as well as minds. Often, people respond to conversations about inequity and privilege by contracting physically. The rigidity people feel in their bodies makes it harder for them to think flexibly. When teams calls on themselves and others to confront systematic barriers and create equitable response across organizations and communities, it's helpful for members to be present, grounded, and open in both mind and body. This energizes their work with others, empowering them to address the inequities built into rules, policies, and laws. Building the mind and body to handle unfamiliar conversations means teams can address the most difficult problems in their world. They become a team that embodies bravery.

Here is where Dana's team's investment of time in the invitation and the onboarding conversations made a huge difference. The core and change teams built commitment to the shared promise and to each other. These commitments proved strong enough to keep teammates listening to and learning from each other through uncomfortable conversations.

MAKING OUR DIVERSITY WORK FOR US

Kenyatta T. Brunson
PRESIDENT AND CHIEF EXECUTIVE OFFICER
N STREET VILLAGE

At N Street Village, we believe every woman deserves a home.

We're a team of seven people who build programs and deliver services to benefit homeless women from traumatic backgrounds. Some of us have over 15 years of experience working with individuals experiencing homelessness; others have none. Some are focused on the narrative we could tell; others are concerned about the mechanics of interventions to help end homelessness. Some focus on policies; others are moved by the people. Some are older; others are Millennials. Some are Black; others, White. While our team is diverse, it was not a *well-functioning* diverse team.

We had to learn to trust each other—to trust that we had good intentions and all wanted the same thing: to end homelessness for women. To do this, we needed to be intentional about building on our diversity to work for us and for the mission of the organization.

Working with Steven Jones showed me that when the team is working well, we're making a promise to each other and the work. Steven encouraged me to think about our collective promise *to each other.* I began having biweekly meetings with the team, where we discussed our collective promise to *each other* and to the women we serve. We worked to define that promise in open conversations.

Together, we grew from a frustrated group to a high-functioning team. We learned to give each other the space to be unique. Each day, we strive to be more culturally competent as a team, as well as in our work. We recognize that the diversity of our team brings us what we need to continue to grow.

TEAM PRACTICES FOR INCLUSION

These teams were diverse by design. They had committed to building equity, which in this case means enabling fair access to a long and healthy life. They also had committed to inclusion—ensuring that all people, especially those who have been historically marginalized, feel welcomed to participate with an equal voice. The teams developed specific practices to sustain inclusion. For example, they took the time to prepare for challenging conversations by pausing and breathing. Team leaders met periodically with individuals and small groups to stay connected and support everyone in being heard.

Dana's team created environments where:

- All voices were honored and respected.
- People were recognized and valued for their contributions.
- The team made space for people who had not always belonged to bring their gifts.
- Once people were engaged equitably, the team supported each other to thrive as contributors to achieving the shared promise.

In committing to inclusion, they were not just being "nice." Rather, they were challenging unconscious bias for the sake of accessing the full brilliance of their community. Bias prompts an unspoken question that people in the majority culture may ask themselves when someone from a non-privileged group joins the team: "Will you have anything truly valuable to offer? Is it worth listening to you?" Challenging these beliefs requires learning spaces where people can see, "This is a place where I have a bit of bias. It's a long-standing cultural bias that I didn't create, but I've absorbed it. Now, I have the opportunity to interrupt it."

Committed teams explore the ways they may not listen to someone they don't yet trust. A team member can then say, "I think you're having trouble hearing our colleague. Let's regroup and then go back. I invite you to listen with curiosity and respect to their experiences and insights." Team members listen and summarize, synthesize, build on, or inquire into what they've heard from their colleagues—especially those who may not have been heard historically.

Dana and the core team committed to inclusion as a game-changer on three levels, as we've described in the *Foundations* sidebar as ME—WE—WORLD.[69] At each level, the old game[70] perpetuated exclusion rather than belonging for those in non-privileged races, while the new game addresses racial equity. At the **World** level, Dana's initiative aimed to change the systemic experiences that shorten lives of Black community members. At the **We** level, they changed the game by rethinking who gets to speak for and lead change in this city. At the **Me** level, they invited each team member to wade into challenging conversations about identity and inequity—not by throwing anyone in the deep end, but by supporting each other in learning to swim in deeper waters.

The teams examined the structures and practices that sustain their city's culture through a racial lens. Together they asked: To what should we pay attention so we see can how inequity resides in our community? How do our practices attribute benefits and privileges to one group of people while limiting or denying those same benefits to others? Which people have or lack access to opportunities that build health? What outcomes are produced by the historical way of thinking? What is the cost—in human and financial suffering—as well as the wasted potential? What results might we create if we thought differently?

In the time since Dana launched this promise, these teams have made consistent progress. The change team created agreement among the city's leaders, businesses, and other entities that racial life span disparity exists and needs to be eradicated. Though the pandemic slowed action, team members persisted. They are now creating agreements with a coalition of city leaders to develop policies and programs in areas most likely to matter to the health of their marginalized communities, including high-quality childcare, affordable housing, and education practices to close the achievement gap.

CREATING YOUR OWN BRAVE AND INCLUSIVE TEAM

What do you care about for yourself and your world? What could be a more inclusive and equitable future for your community? What could you accomplish with a diverse and brave team?

As you build that team, perhaps Dana's experience can provide guidance:

- Become clear on a specific future that matters to you and others.

- Find data that describe the current situation and benefits of the future you envision.

- Ask people who share your care to begin designing this with you.

- Check who is missing. Invite those diverse community members to join you.

> *Welcome and include people in ways that bring forward all voices, insights, and gifts.*

- Welcome and include people in ways that bring forward all voices, insights, and gifts.

- Build one or more teams where people are committed to a shared promise and to hear, support, and bring out the best in each other.

- Stay aware of the emotional experience of your team. Make space for speaking concerns and hopes, so you can design with the entire community in mind—not just majority perspectives.

- Open yourself to learning in the face of challenging conversations about race.

- Keep focus on the valuable future you're creating while staying flexible about how to accomplish that future.

- Regularly assess your progress in creating results, and determine next steps together.

As more people in our society awaken to racial injustices, we see the opportunity for people to work together to make change in their communities and organizations. This doesn't mean change is inevitable—it's just more possible. You set the conditions for change by developing yourself and others as observers of inequity, and as actors who welcome important conversations—however uncomfortable. By building teams that are diverse, inclusive, and brave, you create a more just world.

RECOMMENDED ACTIONS

- **Engage as a learner.** Let go of the idea that you must have all the correct answers before inviting people to conversations. Stay open to hearing views that may be different from what you expect.

- **Strengthen yourself as an observer of racial and other inequities.** Often, this requires seeking out a broader network of people and opening more meaningful and challenging conversations. Notice when you and others are privileging Whiteness and other forms of racial privilege, and learn to engage all community members with respect and openness.

- **Work with your own stories and emotions about race.** Observe where you live emotionally around the topics of race, racism, and being anti-racist.[71] Be willing to explore anger, fear, guilt, or shame if these come up for you. When entering new or awkward conversations about race, find your center. Touch your stomach and breathe deeply. Feel the air as it enters your lungs. Slowly exhale as you invite yourself to this opportunity for learning.

- **Invite others to join you in creating and owning initiatives.** An essential aspect of a leader's work is to identify their cares and to take a stand to address them. Whenever you take bold stands for something that matters to people beyond yourself, you'll want to make space for others to join you. Your commitment to inclusion means your teams become a springboard for building a more equitable world.

UNITING REMOTE LEADERS INTO TEAMS

Dan Winter

- How do you build a team from leaders used to focusing on "their" part of the organization?

- How do you sustain a team when members are separated by distance and cultures?

- How do you build pride and commitment in an organization that is geographically and culturally distant from headquarters?

Kelly took a slow breadth and said, "We've just committed to double revenue with more products, and we're adding more sites in more countries. How can I double the capabilities of my leaders—and myself? And how do I develop and focus my leadership team when we're spread all over the globe?"

The company had invested in management development for many years. There were weeklong programs for new managers, ongoing classes to help managers drive processes and increase efficiency, and a culture that reinforced the importance of managing teams to produce reliable results. Because products and processes were relatively stable, they had not invested substantially in developing leaders capable of designing new solutions and leading changing organizations. This gap was now being felt by experienced managers facing new leadership challenges in meeting the CEO's call for new products and massive growth.

"We've committed to double revenue with more products, and we're adding more sites in more countries. How can I double the capabilities of my leaders—and myself? And how do I develop and focus my leadership team when we're spread all over the globe?"

Kelly led finance for a global business unit in a Fortune-50 company, and his organization would have to scale. He knew that meant more than hiring faster and racing through more tasks. It meant building organizations and developing people. They needed to pull together across three continents and six cultures to develop solutions to drive growth. To succeed, he and his leaders would have to stretch their capabilities, starting with his staff of direct reports, each of whom managed large functional groups.

To succeed in doubling revenue, Kelly knew he needed more than a loosely connected group committed to satisfying him as their boss. He needed a team committed to the overall goal and to helping each other transform the organization.

PREPARING TO BUILD A TEAM

Growing a team when the members are separated by distance, time zones, and cultures can be especially difficult, so the fundamentals of teamwork become especially important:

- Establish a shared sense of purpose that meets the various needs of the members.

- Define a shared future that draws the members together and reinforces the most productive behaviors.

- Evoke a mood of optimism and positive engagement for change.

- Create a rhythm of practices to lead, coach, and drive results.

- Build trust within the team and between the team and its partners.

When Kelly and I met, we started with a conversation about care. The executives above Kelly had said several times that they didn't want to waste time and money on "training" when there was "real work" to be done, and he was keenly aware of the risk he faced. We wanted to ensure the hard work ahead to scale his team and his own leadership was meaningful, satisfying, and successful:

- What made this challenge worth three years of his life?

- What made the future he wanted to create here more worthwhile than any of the other business challenges he could choose?

- What would it take for team members at all levels to choose to invest their time and effort to scale the business?

- How would this address the priorities of Kelly's boss and executive leadership?

Through this discussion, we established a solid foundation from which Kelly could lead his team. Kelly cared about growing the people in his organization. His organization had succeeded by growing employees internally from recent college graduates into leadership positions. He felt a personal sense of fulfillment in developing people's capabilities, and he considered many to be friends as well as colleagues.

Kelly loved the company and wanted it to be incredibly successful. He wanted the teams in countries where his organization operated to be successful as well. His group frequently was one of the first Western or multinational companies to go into these locations. They motivated local governments to invest in schools and infrastructure, which benefitted entire communities over time. Kelly also saw leading the growth of the organization and increased business results as a path to grow his own scope and prove himself to corporate leadership.

We then started to frame the change. We already knew the production and delivery goals, but how did the organization need to change? What was the future Kelly was trying to create, and how was that different from where the organization was today?

Growth would require innovation, not just execution. It would require risk-taking and investment in new ways of working. The company needed to accelerate the development of the skills and experiences needed to fill critical, expanding roles. They could then hire more local people and begin to build their skills. Kelly needed his staff to operate more cohesively, creating innovative solutions together to work as a global organization—not just within sites and regions—and he needed support from leaders above him to allow them to try new approaches and deepen investments in their people.

Prepared with a grounded sense of purpose, Kelly decided to use his next staff meeting to bring the group together to face the challenge of massive growth. We wanted to understand how they had interpreted the company's vision and where they saw themselves connected to this future. Kelly aimed to expand his perspective, identify where there were unique concerns or misunderstandings within the group, and create the needed buy-in and commitment from the team as they created a shared care for the future. By the end of the discussion, he wanted them to see this as a shared challenge they were choosing—rather than one Kelly had forced on them.

INVITING STAFF TO FORM A COMMITTED TEAM

Holding this conversation virtually wasn't ideal, but we couldn't wait until their next face-to-face meeting. We set ground rules to make it safe for staff members to express their hopes and concerns. We didn't want shallow promises and head-nodding support for "the boss." We wanted to make sure we heard the stories they were carrying about what was important, what was possible, what was fair, and, most of all, how they saw themselves in creating the future.

Kelly started with his appreciation for the team—his story about who they were and why they were chosen for this team. He reminded them he had been very deliberate in hiring each of them, because he saw their capabilities, potential, and commitment to lead—not just manage—their organizations. He was clear and heartfelt in communicating his appreciation for everything they had contributed so far to make the organization successful, and how much he enjoyed being their leader. He also noted his own need to grow as a leader and that he did not have all the answers himself.

The team members had all heard the CEO's call to double revenue. Kelly spent time with each team member to hear what they took away from the CEO's call to action. What opportunities and problems did this open in their minds? What assumptions did they have about headwinds and tailwinds that might impact their progress? What did they see as the most important challenges to address? What was their view of the future? What needed to be different to create the future to which they aspired? How might they each need to grow as leaders?

A relief that we were in this together as a team—instead of each leader approaching this seemingly insurmountable challenge on their own.

Throughout the process, Kelly and I asked clarifying questions. He offered support and reinforcement. He listened for moods of resignation or neutral acceptance, and leaned in with questions when these showed up. He shared his own sense of the value and purpose of this work to draw them into a mood of possibility. By the end of the meeting, we had created a common understanding of the challenge, significant alignment on what it would take to meet it, and a relief that we were in this together as a team—instead of each leader approaching this seemingly insurmountable challenge on their own.

The team committed to three shared priorities:

- Change how the organization did business—driving a cross-site approach to managing and leading, building networks across regions, and developing and sharing solutions to accelerate change and drive efficiency.

- Develop enthusiasm in the organization—having employees see the organization as a great place to grow their careers and ignite a passion for collaborating through unprecedented change.

- Prepare people to lead across an expanding number of sites by developing more powerful coaching capabilities and building clearer models of "soft" skills, so emerging managers and leaders could better see what greatness looks like.

Importantly, we started a map of the conversations needed for us to make this happen. With this grounded, shared sense of the goal, the next conversation asked team members to explore three questions related to accomplishing the priorities:

- What do we need to be doing differently to create change in these areas? Where do we need to focus our attention, and how do we need to spend our time differently?
- How do we need to be different as leaders?
- What about this will be personally difficult?

CYCLE OF CONVERSATIONS

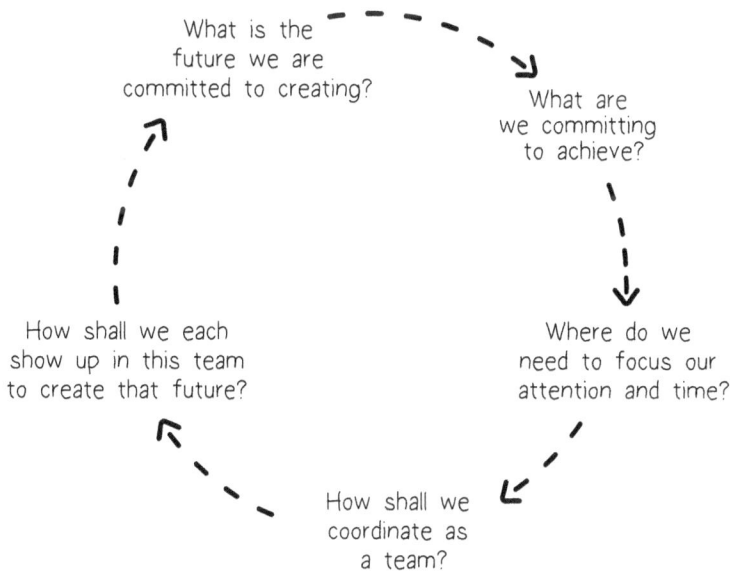

What is the future we are committed to creating?

What are we committing to achieve?

How shall we each show up in this team to create that future?

Where do we need to focus our attention and time?

How shall we coordinate as a team?

From this discussion, they identified several changes in how they would approach the transformation:

- Allocate staff time to discuss progress in developing locals to be leaders both within and across sites.

- Plan specific manager and mentor conversations with employees to clarify what was expected beyond technical excellence to win and be successful in leadership roles.

- As leaders, free up their own time to be more strategic by delegating tasks to emerging leaders to develop skills and experience.

- Create new "right hand" positions to prepare as replacements so that when a team member rotated back to the U.S., there was already a familiar, capable leader embedded to continue the momentum.

- And, perhaps most critically, Kelly needed to open conversations to align the executives of the organization to support these changes.

It was OK to ask for help, to slip back to old habits and then course correct, and to learn from each other.

Throughout this discussion, team members felt included and challenged by ensuring we heard from each—without letting any single voice dominate, and without closing discussions until everyone was heard. Team members realized that scaling would require growth—they would have to give up comfortable, familiar, proven habits and get fully engaged in their personal and shared learning. They would have to withstand the vulnerability and discomfort of experimenting with new ways of leading, in front of each other. We created a shared understanding that struggling with this was a normal part of leadership. It was OK to ask for help, to slip back to old habits and then course correct, and to learn from each other.

ACCELERATING TRUST

We took advantage of an upcoming face-to-face meeting to deepen relationships and collaboration. While this group had been on staff together for months or years, for much of that time, they were each leading their respective sites and organizations with a high degree of independence without shared priorities across the organization. We wanted to help them learn how to help each other lead—to move from personal leadership to team leadership.

Our next step was to build the trust needed to identify and resolve breakdowns quickly in honest, supportive conversations. We asked each person to share:

- What was your favorite job and why?
- What significant event most helped establish who you are as a leader?
- What's important for people to know about working with you?
- What do you do exceptionally well that you love doing? What feels fulfilling when people ask for your help?
- What do you struggle to do well and would like to get help or delegate to others?
- What brings out your best as a member of the team?
- What frustrates you most as a member of a team?

The team emerged from this exercise more open and connected to each other. By sharing who they were, who they aspired to be, and why they engaged the way they did, they allowed each other to adopt much more generous interpretations of previously resented behaviors. They were more willing to express themselves and listen to others, and they became more comfortable raising concerns with each other when they felt breakdowns or disconnects. This enabled them to learn together and support each other in pursuit of their common goals. They learned to speak for each other and to advocate to their organizations and partners on behalf of each other. Most importantly, they evolved from being a staff of managers to a team of leaders.

BUILDING BELONGING ON TEAMS ACROSS THE GLOBE

David Schmid
HEAD OF FINANCE, CFO - AWS LATIN AMERICA COMMERCIAL SALES

Leading a rapidly expanding finance team in Chengdu, China, for a multinational company required me to help our local employees learn the company's processes and culture. Dan Winter helped me see I needed to create a larger sense of shared purpose around our goals.

I started with our site motto, "Chengdu Can Do!" and introduced the team to a concept of Ohana from one of my favorite Disney films, *Lilo and Stitch*. Per the film, "Ohana means family. Family means nobody gets left behind or forgotten." We built on this to define goals together, including having the majority of the regional finance lead positions based at our site with local leaders in all but one position, which would save more than $1 million dollars per year.

We created our own "school" for finance people, including a graduation ceremony with caps and gowns. The curriculum focused heavily on topics that were critical to the global organization, but not covered by local universities. This includes Critical Thinking, How to Disagree and Commit, Business Partnering, and Economics. They joined cross-site functional teams that worked on process and operational improvements. This helped the local teams see themselves as members of the larger global Ohana, building professional and personal relationships with people they seldom met in person.

Whenever possible, I sent key team members to other sites to attend conferences and meet face-to-face with their peers. The key, I found, was to have them debrief with the rest of the team so everyone got to know the rest of the global Ohana. With our focus as a family, we found our "graduates" quickly became site leaders and then regional leaders.

TRANSFORMING THE ORGANIZATION TO SUCCEED AT SCALE

Now the hard work of organizational transformation began. The team developed a global approach to managing employee development. Instead of developing employees at each site, they looked across the global organization, set standards for roles at various levels, and built the expectation to operate regionally and globally into promotion criteria. Team members looked for opportunities to accelerate employee growth through international assignments and global roles.

*Members worked to build relationships by
co-leading initiatives and role modeling
this partnership to their organizations.*

Kelly's team began reaching out to each other for ideas and support where local resources were insufficient. Each member learned to look to the team to help accelerate results, worrying less about who would get credit or which site was doing best and more about how they could get great results, so that everyone could benefit. Members worked to build relationships by co-leading initiatives, and role modeling this partnership to their organizations.

In addition to the formal work, the team built a practice of personal connection. When team members were at the same site, they had many small, informal, personal discussions. Coffee breaks, hallway discussions, and pre-meeting discussions all provided a chance to catch up, reconnect, and share insights that build relationships. Since Kelly's team operated remotely, the members built an informal cadence of calls, including virtual lunches and coffee breaks, to connect on non-work topics, such as how their kids were doing with the start of school, interesting vacation or travel stories, classes, or speaking events they had attended. This built camaraderie and commonality, driving connection beyond immediate tasks.

Over time, Kelly's team transformed the organization, developing local hires into leadership positions, helping employees at all levels learn to operate as part of cross-site, global teams, and building strong coaching and development throughout the organization. As each rotated back to positions in the U.S. or their home site, they stayed connected, helping those who remained and those who replaced them to continue to grow and develop the organization and each other, while building bridges back to leaders at the headquarters. Kelly and his team deliberately chose new members who were committed to the team's challenges and integrated them through many of the same conversations they had gone through earlier—setting clear expectations that they were all learning together.

The organization succeeded in meeting impressive growth targets, and Kelly's team members were in high demand. Most went on to become VPs and CFOs in this company and at others, bringing with them the commitment and practices to build teams where people belong, grow, and deliver results.

RECOMMENDED ACTIONS

- **Build the team's foundation.** Dispersed teams, like all teams, need a solid foundation. If the foundation isn't in place, dispersed teams feel the effects even more than those who are co-located. Ensure everyone is heard as you create a shared goal to which you are all committed.

- **Create personal connection.** Intentionally create time to connect beyond the work at hand. This could be quick, informal check-ins, sharing stories about family events, or celebrating life events. Even virtual coffee breaks can help members stay connected.

- **Create a safe space for feedback and appreciation.** It's easy to misread intentions and actions, and remote teams have fewer opportunities for immediate feedback, clarification, and correction than co-located teams. Make time for appreciating members, including their different styles and contributions to the team.

- **Pay close attention to moods and meaning.** It's easy to misread the mood and tone across differing cultures, especially in remote settings. How cultures express conflict, appreciation, and disagreement is likely to be very different and easily misinterpreted by those with less experience working with members of a given culture or community. While dispersed teams will share a common language, the choice and meaning of words may be quite different. Encourage members to check their understanding frequently

IGNITING THE VALUE OF CROSS-GENERATIONAL TEAMS

Heather Neely

- What strengths and assumptions do I bring to this team as a member of my generation?

- What benefits can we draw from the mix of generations on our team?

- What conversations are important for our team so we can make the most of our generational diversity?

"I look forward to seeing all of you back in the office every day!" exclaimed one of our client CEOs.

Another implored, "Directors and vice presidents, please come in person whenever you can."

In 2021 and 2022, we saw CEOs across industries and countries request, demand, and cajole their staff to return to the traditional five-day workweek in the office. Exhausted and worried after pandemic disruptions and relentless market expectations, leaders wanted to bring their teams back to the office to coordinate more easily, evaluate and develop their staff, boost morale, and drive results.

This call was met with mixed reactions, from enthusiasm to compliance to looking for other work. People across the generational spectrum voiced their hesitancy to return to the office five days a week. This was particularly true of members of the Millennial Generation (born 1981–1996). While many employees had adjusted to working from home, it was younger workers and parents who seemed most delighted that the business world had finally embraced remote work as a productive option.

This same drama unfolded at several of our clients, and we facilitated conversations between leaders and employees to address their full range of concerns. The leaders, mainly from the Baby Boomer and Generation X generations, were skeptical about achieving consistent results remotely, while many Gen Zers and Millennials, who grew up with technology, felt confident they could produce the same or better work without commuting and office distractions. After much dialogue, our clients found middle paths that met the needs of both the company and the evolving workforce.

SEEING THE GENERATION GAP

This type of "generational mismatch" is not new. Two decades ago, I was asked by a Fortune 500 company to help "rein in" the Generation X workers in their customer-facing call center. The managers, who were Baby Boomers, complained that young workers left after a year, were overly eager to acquire skills, and were not willing to put in the time to "pay their dues."

After talking with several leaders, I spoke to the employees themselves. The Gen Xers said that these "old school" people were limiting their careers—blocking them from learning and bringing their talent to the broader company. They saw their call center job as a great introduction to the company, but once the learning curve flattened, they wanted to be able to move to more challenging departments.

The Gen Xers believed if they weren't actively learning, they were in danger of becoming obsolete. They were growing more and more frustrated with their leaders who didn't have a path forward for them inside the company, and even blocked them from interviewing with other departments. As a result, the Gen Xers stayed a year and then quit—leaving the call center with significant unwanted attrition and costing the company hundreds of thousands of dollars in rehiring and retraining.

It was clear these two distinct generations were completely missing each other's intentions. Many Generation X employees had already experienced corporate layoffs and embraced a free agent mindset: Nimbly acquiring relevant workplace skills was the new job security. The Gen Xers saw their employment as "contractual." They were willing to give their all while they were there, but they needed to stay relevant and on a learning curve at all times in order to feel secure.

The Boomer managers felt they were doing these young workers a great service by offering long-term work with a globally respected company. For Boomers, job security was excelling in your position, climbing the corporate ladder, being patient and loyal, and earning a nice retirement package. However, job security for Gen Xers centered on rapid skill and knowledge acquisition. Gen Xers felt the Boomers were putting them in grave danger by expecting them to stay in a job where the learning curve was not steep enough to keep them marketable. Adding insult to injury, Gen Xers were blocked from interviewing inside the company for opportunities to grow and challenge themselves.

We listened to both the call center leadership team and the employees who reported to them then rolled up our sleeves to help the call center make adjustments. We implemented different tiers in the call center, giving people ways to clearly see the skills they were acquiring at each new level of challenge. We also offered cross-generational workshops to all employees, helping them recognize and address their own unconscious generational biases.

In addition, we worked with managers to see that it was not in the company's best interest to hold people back from interviewing internally. We set standards that employees could be eligible for internal moves after 9–12 months on the job. We worked with internal recruiting, career services, and talent development to help call center employees gain visibility into other departments in the company.

Different generations tend to have different perspectives, gifts, and approaches to work.

The results were astounding. Call center tenure increased, unwanted attrition dropped, and the company had a robust internal pipeline for talent. The lesson here is that different generations tend to have different perspectives, gifts, and approaches to work.[72,73] When we don't explore these, everyone loses.

DIFFERENT GENERATIONS OBSERVE THE WORLD DIFFERENTLY

For decades, it's been clear that people from different generations have "superpowers," strengths that set them up to take action in distinct ways. Most workplace teams are a mix of people from different generations. These differences are observable—obviously or subtly—in how people conduct themselves. The question becomes how we understand these differences and leverage them so that our teams are vibrant, relevant, innovative, and in sync with the ever-changing world.

Each generation is uniquely sculpted by the social, political, and economic circumstances of their lives. Therefore, each generation develops a slightly different lens and toolkit of skills, which they bring to their work. This diverse mix of perspectives and skills means intergenerational teams can innovate and adapt more successfully.

This is also where the generational misunderstandings arise. For example, Generation Xers were labeled early on as slackers who didn't want to pay their dues—a perspective which missed their commitment to growth. People often judge what others are doing without understanding the bigger picture about where and how these differences can be leveraged to understand the whole workforce and their multigenerational customers.

Generation Xers focus on fierce independence and autonomy. They're not willing to pay their dues and climb the corporate ladder for the sake of tradition—especially since many of them had seen widespread layoffs. Boomers pride themselves on their corporate loyalty, collaboration, perseverance, and willingness to pay their dues. You can imagine the tension and frustration between these two genera-tions of people who simply observe the world in distinct ways.

Our job is not to "fix" anyone, but to get everyone talking, so they can see the brilliance in their diversity. We are committed to helping in-tergenerational teams move beyond the hyper-focus of how they are different and to get curious about how to blend their styles to benefit the organization and their own work satisfaction.

Being inclusive starts by understanding that different people are "distinct observers."

Assembling diverse teams is only a start. To perform at truly high lev-els, teams must welcome and in-clude all the diversity on the team. Being inclusive starts by under-standing that different people are "distinct observers."[74] Each person interprets the world differently. These individual interpretations are mediated by many factors, including community dynamics around race, class, and immigration. Because generational experiences broadly shape how we were raised—what our parents argued about, what we were rewarded for in school, what technology we had access to, etc.—generations powerfully shape the observers we've become.

Having different observers on teams brings gifts and challenges. When I think of teams that work skillfully together, they have ways of harvesting the gifts that each brings. To reap the benefits of mul-tigenerational teams, we must become curious about how life events impact other people. We must step outside of our generational lens and look through the lens of others if we're to gain value from diver-sity. Additionally, we can slow down, make fewer assumptions, and ask more questions.

WHO ARE THE GENERATIONS IN THE WORKFORCE TODAY?

Let's discuss four generations in the workforce today—Baby Boomers, Generation X, the Millennial Generation and Gen Z—so you can learn how to ignite conversations that inspire and integrate the best of what each generation can offer.

A generation is defined as a group of people with a shared historical, social, and economic experience. Generational differences have been at play for hundreds of years. It's inevitable that people from different generations have different life experiences and then behave accordingly.

Move beyond stereotypes, judgments, and unproductive moods by intentionally having conversations where we see the possibilities in the diversity.

Part of the friction among generationally diverse people is that the "newest generation" is showing us a snapshot of the future, which can be disorienting. As we see the next generation navigate the workplace, we may question whether we made the best choices for our own careers. We may have feelings of fear that bring us to the edges of our own relevancy. When we as people and teams are stuck in such moods as fear, we don't perform at our best.

One way to improve our teams is to see the generational mix and learn to move beyond stereotypes, judgments, and unproductive moods by intentionally having conversations where we see the possibilities in the diversity.

GENERATIONS SEE THE WORLD DIFFERENTLY

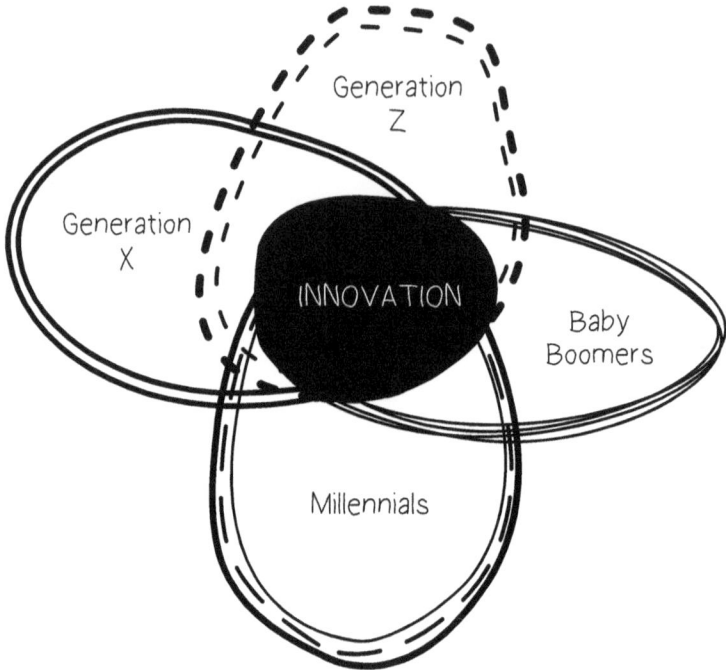

Here is a glimpse of the generational groups found in today's workforce:

Baby Boomers (born between 1946 and 1964)

The Baby Boomers are post–World War II babies who grew up in the disruptive '60s and then the expansions and contractions of the '70s and '80s. As they came of age, their sheer numbers had a tremendous impact on entire industries, including the building of tract housing and the emergence of targeted marketing.

Many Baby Boomers came into the workplace at a time in U.S. history when the expectation was you would spend your entire career in one company or organization. In exchange for your loyalty, your retirement would be covered. Then, Boomers were laid off in droves as corporations scrambled to maintain profit margins, increase market share, and compete globally. The Boomers who survived the layoffs needed to pivot their mindset from being loyal employees to "free agent" employees. For some, this shift was jarring and unexpected, while for others working in this new way brought welcome flexibility and professional opportunities.

Boomers have perspective and context and have seen it all—good and bad. They are, as a generation, a team. They know what "the collective" is and they understand *how* to work and be with others in group settings. They value personal growth, collaboration, and the opportunity to contribute their wisdom.

Generation X (born between 1965 and 1980)

Gen Xers came of age during widespread institutional downfalls of every kind, including the traditional family, political, and government institutions. They were the first "latchkey" generation of children, many of whom were unattended after school, either because both of their parents worked or were divorced.

Xers developed independence and the ability to entertain themselves for hours upon end without supervision. Instead of "corporate" jobs, many Xers worked several part-time jobs. Some started their own businesses, while others found jobs in traditional companies of all sizes. They became the vanguard of the free agent workforce—loyal to themselves, and to others who helped grow their talents.

This is a generation of people with a fierce independence and a free agent mindset. They don't expect corporate loyalty and instead see every work arrangement as contractual. They give their all to the task at hand, and are nimble at accumulating skills that they can transfer to their next work opportunity. Gen Xers both operate independently and enjoy working towards goals in parallel with others. They're used to things changing and being dynamic, so they move easily between jobs and projects. They're not overly concerned with authority, yet work best with clarity of roles. They appreciate a casual work setting that is results-oriented. They focus not on time spent, but on work output.

Millennial Generation (born between 1981 and 1996)

Millennials came of age during economic expansion and are the first generation who claim technology as a birthright. Technology influenced the formation of their identities, their political, social, and cultural views, and their attitudes. Many Millennials were raised by so-called "helicopter parents," who swooped in to protect and guide them at every turn. Millennials are the most culturally diverse generation in U.S. history, and the first to be inclusive of differing lifestyles.

Millennials are members of a global community, and they enjoy collaborative and fun work environments. They're more optimistic than their Generation X counterparts, yet they balance out this optimism with grounded data-driven realism. They're tenacious learners who multitask with more ease than any other generation. Because they grew up with technology, they're perfectly suited for working away from the traditional office. They're digital nomads and will work anytime, anyplace, and at any hour. They require clarity about due dates and clear expectations about final work product.

With technology as a birthright, Millennials understand *how* to use technology in ways that integrate seamlessly into daily life. They tend to welcome diversity and include others without judging. Their optimism is refreshing on a team. They will see what's possible and move to make it happen. Millennials are open to being coached, because they appreciate learning from others, as it has been part of their life experience. Because they were raised to feel valued for their uniqueness, they recognize that the people in a company are what makes a company or organization successful.

Generation Z (born between 1997 and 2013)

Gen Z came into a world in constant disruption, and they will likely be even scrappier than the Millennial Generation. Older Generation Zers will resemble more of the attributes of Generation X, simply because there will likely be far fewer jobs available as they enter the workforce.

We can expect Generation Z to become fierce pioneers, reinventing work and life in the face of simultaneous shocks: the first global pandemic in a century, resulting in massive labor shortages in certain job sectors such as nursing; reckoning with long-standing systemic racial inequity; and the impact that robotics and artificial intelligence will have in replacing or redefining future jobs.

The COVID-19 Pandemic is undeniably this generation's defining event, as 9/11 was for Millennials. "Pandemic life" deprived many Gen Zers of typical social interactions, teen jobs, and a regular school experience. It's difficult to predict the work habits of a generation that is still entering the workforce. But we can already piece together factors to watch.

Gen Z is committed to defining and driving their own excellence. This will likely be one of the hallmarks of this generation, as they continue to come of age during a time of uncertainty and re-invention. Gen Zers are resourceful and creative. They enjoy working independently or alongside others on teams and in work groups. Many of the Gen Zers who enter the professional workforce during the pandemic have been interviewed, hired, and onboarded to work teams without ever shaking someone's hand or meeting anyone in their new company face-to-face.

Gen Z is also even more culturally diverse than the Millennial Generation. They're at the forefront of deepening our understanding of multiculturalism and gender fluidity, and they will continue to re-define the word inclusion.

Gen Z will comprise and shape the Fourth Industrial Revolution, which will include the benefits and disruptions of robotics, artificial intelligence, nanotechnology, and autonomous vehicles. Pay attention to how they push your company to innovate—they have their finger on the pulse of the future.

CREATING A SUCCESSFUL INTERGENERATIONAL TEAM

Gonzalo Peralta

EXECUTIVE DIRECTOR, LANGUAGES CANADA

Diego, a Millennial, left a secure government position to work in a small non-profit where he felt he could make a difference. As long as he is learning, creating, and being compensated fairly, he will stay with the organization. He will most definitely leave if these conditions are not met. Linda, a Boomer, has worked in the same nonprofit since its inception in 1995. She's risen through the ranks, devoted her career to serving the organization and will retire from this group having left a lasting mark. Yet Linda, Diego, and the other team members work incredibly well together and admire each other. How can this be?

Even though our team members come from multiple generations, we're all committed to making a shared impact through our organization. But that's not enough. We also understand and respect each other's personal cares—meaning we appreciate we're each different observers who see the world in distinct ways. We found a way to be both unique individuals and a cohesive unit—a must for any successful intergenerational workplace.

Heather helped me see that leaders who make the most of generational diversity create a flow now required in successful organizations. Working with Pam, my organization was able to see the importance of generations to innovation by tracing our history as we created our strategy. Any successful strategy has to consider the link between past, present, and future—and the valuable contribution each generation makes.

That's why we ask two questions: How will today's twelve-year-olds observe things differently? And, how can we use the contributions of each generation to innovate, generate, and thrive?

WELCOMING CONVERSATIONS FOR INCLUSION

As Altus works with teams, we look at the conversations they need to have in a skillful way in order to coordinate actions to get desired results. The CEO of one of our clients commented that one of the biggest sources of stress at work are the conversations we never have.

Teams seldom make time to explore their generational diversity. In our workshops, I show people how to have this missing generational conversation. The best part is not what I teach people about their generation, but what they share with each other about their generational lens and their generations' strengths and gifts.

My invitation is to find the courage to engage your teams in cross-generational conversations to bring you together and ignite new possibilities, actions, and results!

RECOMMENDED ACTIONS

- **Understand your history.** Bring your generationally diverse teams together to talk about defining events for their generation. Remember to hold these conversations with curiosity instead of certainty and judgment. Ask them to create lists of what defining events they experience, and ask them to reflect on how those defining events helped to shape how they see the world and how they approach their daily work. This exercise allows people to share their distinct points of view and see their collective strengths.

- **Talk about how this impacts current team dynamics.** Invite your generationally diverse teams to explore the team's strengths and blind spots from their generational lenses. How do these show up in your team today? You might look at technical strengths, personal practices, networks, and communication channels.

- **Build your future together.** From the respect you've built with the previous conversations, guide the team to consider how to draw more fully on their strengths. Ask how each team member wants to grow as they move through this phase of their lives and careers. Make space to consider how the team can support them in growing. Consider cross-generational mentorships for generating even more intentional learning and growing.

- **Extend your team learnings to deepen customer insight.**
  These team conversations make it easier to talk about
  generational differences with understanding and compassion,
  instead of stereotypes. Invite your generationally inclusive team
  to update products, services, and communications to serve the
  diversity of your customers.

BECOMING CAPABLE OF BUILDING SUCCESSFUL TEAMS

OUR CEO IS BLOCKING TEAM SUCCESS (AND I'M THE CEO)

Andrea Bordenca

- As a leader, what is my role, and where may I be getting in the way of my team?

- How does my own growth as a person and leader improve team performance?

- How can I lead in ways that help my team to grow as well?

The company was at a crossroads. Revenue and profitability were stagnant, and the founder needed to step down for health reasons. Would the next CEO be able to work through the problems and transform the organization into a vibrant and growing business?

This is more than just a case study—it's personal. The company, Diagnostic Equipment Service Corporation (DESCO), was started by my father. I was the successor whose leadership was in question.

I had worked for DESCO in various support roles throughout the years, so I thought I knew what the company needed. My vision was to grow it beyond the small, regional entity my father had cultivated for 35 years. However, like many other new leaders, I didn't know what I didn't know—about the business, about the team, and, most importantly, about myself as a leader.

As I started at the helm, I didn't stop to ask our employees for input. My approach was, "I'm in a leadership role, so I tell people what to do. They may not like all of it, but that's what they need to do." I thought my job was to be the expert—crystal clear and very directive.

In addition to driving strategy, my mental model of "leader as expert" had me diving in to learn more about electronics and mechanics, as if I were going to advise experienced technicians on fixing medical equipment. Instead of drawing on the team's experience, I spent time trying to catch up with their decades of knowledge.

As I focused on becoming technically proficient, business results slid downhill. Employee turnover and customer defections increased. Revenue and profitability declined. My attempts to lead as an expert weren't working—something had to change.

EXAMINING MY DEFINITION OF LEADERSHIP

I had equated effective leadership with knowing a lot about our products and market, and working very, very hard. I wanted to be an "A+" CEO, so I did what most of us learned to do in school—work hard, cram knowledge into my brain, and show that I knew stuff. But DESCO already had team members who understood electronics and mechanics, and they already worked very hard. What we didn't have was an effective leader.

Because I was determined to be a better CEO, I began studying with the Institute for Generative Leadership (IGL). I discovered that my unexamined definition of leadership was just one way to look at it— and not a very useful one. My approach neither motivated my team nor gave me the benefit of their wisdom and experience.

My business needed a CEO who could see what conversations we needed to take the business forward.

At IGL, I came to see that effective leaders engage people in building futures that matter—to employees and customers, as well as to the leaders. I discovered that leaders build futures through conversations. My business needed a CEO who could see what conversations we needed to take the business forward—conversations about the changing needs of our customers, how we allocate capital, and how we retain and grow our team members.

So, I started paying attention to my speaking and listening. Soon I recognized a pattern: I often jumped into solving the apparent problem without listening for other perspectives. I wasn't inviting people to reflect on what was and wasn't working, nor was I creating space for learning and improving. Instead, I invented solutions and told the team what we were going to do. As a result, people stopped using their own observations and expertise to make the company better, and some disengaged and left.

DRIVING THE COMPANY FORWARD

We've all heard of blind spots—the parts of the road you can't see when changing lanes. Early on, I didn't realize that my blind spots as a leader could cause my team to crash. In fact, my blind spots would certainly cause problems for my team unless I worked on expanding what I saw and sincerely inviting my team to show me what I was missing.

When I made time to reflect on my own learning to share with my employees, I discovered three patterns:

- I saw myself as the decider rather than an orchestra conductor. Accordingly, I was not listening or inviting the wisdom, insights, and skills of our team members.

- I worked painfully hard and dared others to match me. As a result, we all became exhausted and frustrated.

- I thought I was supposed to be constantly cheery and pretend I wasn't frustrated and exhausted. This made it hard for all of us to be honest about problems. Consequently, it took even more time for me and my team to figure out how we could work effectively together.

I came to see that since the market was always evolving, and the company was always needing to change as a result, no matter how much I learn I will *always* have blind spots. Everyone else on my team will have blind spots, too. Some might miss how service needs are changing in their region; others might miss opportunities to advance our technical capabilities or handle our logistics more efficiently.

No matter how much I learn I will always have blind spots.

This, for me, was the beginning of seeing the beauty of teams.

My job as CEO wasn't to be the perfect driver but to point us in the right direction, build commitment to taking care of our customers, and ensure we had constructive discussions as we navigated. By actively practicing sharing my own learning and modeling this for others, I created a safe space that allows teammates to move from the pressure of perfectionism to the power of sharing our diverse perspectives and building solutions together.

EMBRACING CHANGE, STARTING WITH ME

I usually faced the challenge of a changing market with courage and willingness to try new things, forging my way forward. Sometimes, I contracted in fear; to my team, this probably looked like stress and frustration. For many years, I was not aware even of the triggers and mindsets that provoked my reactions. I just did my best and tried not to look frustrated.

To achieve better results for the company, I needed to see my own gaps in leading the team. My first step was becoming a student of *me*.

I became a student of my reactions. I learned that when I was uncertain, I would become full of doubt and fear. I noticed I would then fall back on what worked for me before, which was often blaming others and resenting others—as if I had no role in any of it.

For example, our status meetings and action meetings would collapse into one another, and the leadership team would lose track of priorities and outcomes. I'd react in the moment and scramble to make the meetings useful, which didn't often happen because I wasn't always clear, and I hadn't led the team to co-create effective prioritization systems and meeting practice. Winging it wasn't working. Worse, the lack of simple structure put me even more in the mode of telling people what to do.

I discovered that my patterns—of acting like the expert, working relentlessly, and not knowing how to navigate my emotions—inhibited my employees from speaking up and making useful offers to build the business.

After making a regular practice of observing and reflecting on the links between my actions and outcomes, I could see that success was not just luck, timing, and hard work: there were skills I could learn and apply.

LEADING THROUGH CONVERSATIONS

A key practice for leaders is engaging productively in different types of conversations, such as conversations for action, possibility, innovation, and relationships. As I learned to design and navigate conversations intentionally—and observe the impact on the team—I figured out how to shift my three patterns. Small shifts in my behavior and mindset produced big results.

I started making space by letting people know that I was open to hearing their perspectives. Instead of telling people what to do, I became willing to say, "I don't know, but here's what I see. What do you see?" I learned to stop working so hard to figure out the answer and instead ask for help. Instead of being falsely cheery, I started saying, "I'm concerned, and I could use your input."

By asking for and making the most of input, I was able to show employees that my commitment was not to dictate our future but to shape it together. Over time, I learned how to engage team members in identifying opportunities together, co-designing, determining the next actions, and generating shared commitment to implementing our decisions.

As I shared my own learning edges,
team members began to share theirs.

As I shared my own learning edges, team members began to share theirs. This meant we could learn and practice together. For example, when we needed to design a new fulfillment process to drive higher customer satisfaction, we set new practices. We created a cross-functional design team to draw on the power of multiple perspectives. We committed to listening to each other, and we shared our experiences about how we listen to each other. We kept learning as we worked together, thoughtfully talking through different scenarios to tackle fulfillment gaps.

In the 20 years since I began working with IGL, DESCO has more than doubled our revenue and gone from operating at a loss to sustaining a net profit. We've been able to transform DESCO into a national organization that has expanded into new markets and continues to grow through customer referrals as well as acquisitions. My growth—shifting these patterns—was crucial in enabling DESCO's team to deliver these results.

These conversations at DESCO continue. We have task forces whose objectives are to improve service, organizational culture, or business development. Because we've all grown in asking questions, listening, and thinking together, these conversations happen without me present. My team continues to see things I never would have seen by myself. This allows me to focus on customers, strategy, and a trustworthy cadence of conversations with all our stakeholders.

MY JOB AS CEO IS TO

Listen and point us in the right direction

Build commitment

Ensure we have constructive discussions

Share my own learnings and model this for others

Create a safe space for teammates to contribute and grow

So we can build solutions together

CHOOSING HEALTHIER WAYS TO LEAD

It's no secret that stress causes health-related issues. Over time, the hormones emitted by stress have short, medium, and long-term effects on overall mental, physical, and emotional well-being. In his book, *The Body Keeps the Score*, Bessel van der Kolk remarks, "The insidious effects of constantly elevated stress hormones include memory and attention problems, irritability, and sleep disorders. They also contribute to many long-term health issues."[75]

My pattern of overworking and always taking on more was my way of showing I was valuable. My family, most schools, and our American business culture are glad to reinforce this mentality. Though it sounds good in the moment—"no one works harder than Andrea!"—the medium- and long-term results were lousy for the business and for me. With overwork, my mental, physical, and emotional health started to break down. I was resigned and resentful.

Had I continued on the same track, I have no doubt I'd be dealing with hypertension, kidney issues, addiction, and other health issues that are common in my family. Because of the stress I carried early in that role, I wasn't sleeping well, I indulged in alcohol nightly, and I was on four different prescriptions for anxiety and attention deficit hyperactivity disorder (ADHD). As I reflected on my leadership, I came to see that my ways of coping did get me through some of life's early challenges, but they were damaging to me, my teams, and my business.

I believed being "in command" was somehow required to be successful. I feared that if people realized I didn't know all the answers, my identity as a leader would be compromised.

I sacrificed personal relationships and health, which made me even less effective. Exhausted and isolated, I sometimes responded sharply to my team and then felt ashamed. Now as I guide other CEOs and teams on their own development journey, I've discovered that this feeling of shame is something other leaders experience. Many of us have absorbed cultural beliefs that work and professional goals must come at the expense of health and relationships as the only way to financial stability and success.

As I've learned to lead from care, honesty, and commitment, I no longer self-medicate with alcohol or anything else, and I manage stress much more effectively. Not only am I healthier, my team members are also healthier with a CEO who shows up with connection, clarity, and curiosity, instead of demands, blame, and stress.

SELF-CARE IS TEAM-CARE

Donna Haghighat, JD
CEO, THE WOMEN'S FUND OF WESTERN MASSACHUSETTS

When we open ourselves to learning, we grow. When we are willing to be seen learning, we inspire team members to grow themselves.

I am reminded of this every time I get to team with Andrea. Andrea Bordenca is a successful two-company CEO and community leader, because she prioritizes her own learning. She asks questions, listens to people's concerns and insights, and builds real commitment to team goals. Andrea recognizes that her individual growth benefits her teams. Beyond sharing content and know-how, her curiosity conveys the value she places on learning.

Because of my learning with Andrea, I have actionable ways to deepen my presence and connection to others by tuning into my breath, paying attention to my mood and to my physical body.

CEOs don't often talk about self-care, yet effective CEOs like Andrea understand that self-care is team-care. We cannot attend to the needs of others—nor can we empower others—when we arrive depleted, anxious, or scattered. Sometimes I've seen gendered stereotypes make it difficult for women to engage in self-care without a strong sense of guilt: What else should I be doing? Whose needs should I be attending to first? The good news is this propensity to put ourselves last can be unlearned.

When we share that—for whatever reason—we are arriving to a team conversation at less than full capacity, we convey to others that we, too, are works in progress and very human. If we can do this with a little levity, it relays that while serious things can happen, we can see the humor as well as the imperfection. Our individual vulnerability and appetite to learn make space for everyone on our teams to show up openly and grow together.

EMBRACING DELIBERATE PRACTICE

My learning from the Institute for Generative Leadership revealed that my propensity to push hard had become a habituated response. The good news about habits is that new ones can be formed with deliberate practice. I now know that history need not dictate how I behave moving forward. I am now at choice. If there are results in life with which I am not satisfied, I choose to learn new ways of responding.

Awareness creates choice is a core generative leadership principle introduced through the somatic teachings of Dr. Richard Strozzi-Heckler.[76] It's been studied in the fields of psychology, psychotherapy, neurobiology, and somatics among such leading researchers and educators as Wilhelm Reich, Elsa Gindler, Moshe Feldenkrais, and Thomas Hanna, as well as Bessel van der Kolk,[77] a pioneer who has led the charge to create new and healthier ways of navigating stress, including trauma.

Shifting from one behavior to another can feel awkward. We need practice to allow the body to learn and absorb the new behavior. The science of neuroplasticity[78] explains how we can create new behavioral practices. When we're aware of our blind spots and are clear that we want to produce a new outcome, we can engage in practices to get there.

My new practice is centering, becoming present to this moment. In an activity-based culture, people can become accustomed to moving from one thing to the next without becoming aware of thoughts, emotions, or tension. I now see that the more I stop to notice what's going on, the more choices I have in the moment. I've come to love this antidote to reacting in anger or frustration.

My learning from the Institute for Generative Leadership was so powerful that several years ago I offered to lead the organization and bring this opportunity to more leaders. So for several years I served as CEO of DESCO, Managing Partner of IGL, and an active contributor in my community—and I do this without the overwhelm, isolation, and frustration I previously carried. Taking care of my development as a leader and a person has brought me the ability to lead teams to greater success in ways that are healthy for all of us.

RECOMMENDED ACTIONS

- **Ask questions before diving into solutions.** Many of us become executives because of our ability to solve problems. By asking questions, we show our teams a framework for thinking together productively:

    - What do you see here? What's at stake for the company and our customers?

    - What are three possibilities that could address this issue?

    - What would a good resolution look like?

- **Walk into the unknown *with* your team.** For your team to create a future that matters to your customers, they must thrive in the ambiguity of exploring options, seeing possibilities, and designing new products and approaches. You cannot save them from uncertainty by pretending to know more than you do. What you can do is show up calm, committed, and curious, and create a team culture where people share their concerns, acknowledge their learning edges, and think through opportunities together.

- **Notice the mood.** Notice in conversations where impatience or frustration show up in you and your team. By paying attention, you will see more possibilities to take empowered action.

    Noticing will enable you to see reactions that have become automatic and embodied from past experiences. We have the power to learn new skills at any age. It's a matter of awareness, choice, and deliberate practice.

- **Share leadership.** Many leaders are the glue or the container that keeps people aligned and work on track. Not only is that a burden for you as the leader, but it usually keeps your team from collaborating effectively. Instead, be clear on the outcome and give your team the runway to think things through and develop the path forward.

- **Check in regularly with your team members.** Be in touch
  on a dependable cadence to think together, offer support, and
  answer questions. Many leaders fear time with their team will give
  the impression team members are not capable or trustworthy.
  Checking in with openness and care does the opposite—it shows
  that you're supporting others on their path.

  You might talk about what you're learning, as well as asking what
  others are learning or want to learn. This is an opportunity for
  team members to identify and speak about areas where they
  feel unsure or have only partial information. Together, as a team,
  you can work to build clarity and expand skills. Conversations are
  your opportunity to build trust, surface and address issues, and
  encourage growth.

GROWING AN AMAZING TEAM FROM SCRATCH

What We've Learned Building Altus Growth Partners

Kobe Bogaert, with Altus Core Team Amy, Dan, Heather, Jan Irene, Juliana, Pam, and Steven

- How do you start a team from scratch?
- How do you get great results and positive work culture?
- How do shared values sustain a team through ups and downs?

> *"Nobody is perfect but a team can be."*
>
> —Meredith Belbin

I was talking with my friend Bill, who owns and runs a financial services company. He was complaining about how hard it was to grow the business. He felt stuck with people who seemed to be there only for a paycheck and didn't help each other provide the quality service he expected.

This is exactly the opposite of the experience I have with our Altus Growth team. At Altus, each team member knows why they are here:

to guide people to have the conversations they need to produce exceptional organizational results and thrive. We each know we do this best in close collaboration as a team. This means team meetings are filled with energy and connection, as we each bring the joy of producing results that matter with people we deeply enjoy.

Building a team that produces great results while enjoying the ride didn't happen by accident. This was our commitment.

It's not that we're perfect—far from it. It's not that we haven't had our struggles—we have—and I expect we'll have more of them in the future. It's not that we have it all figured out—we are endlessly testing improvements to how we operate.

Yet, we have created an amazing team. We feel it, and our clients feel it as they see us working seamlessly together to support their organizations.

Building a team that produces great results while enjoying the ride didn't happen by accident. This was our commitment, and we take action week after week to make good on that commitment. These are actions you can take with your teams, too.

What do we do that has shaped and sustained our amazing team?

We start with care, and we keep checking that we are taking care of what matters to us.

Care is the foundational expression of your authentic intentions in the world.[79] It's what impels you to build a certain kind of future for yourself, your family, and your community.

You might care deeply that kids learn in ways that inspire them, or that people of all socioeconomic conditions have clean air to breathe, or that your family experiences a certain standard of living and well-being. As we each become clear on our fundamental cares, we can choose to take action to take care of those cares.

CARE

is The Foundational Expression

of your authentic
intentions in the

It's what impels you to build
a certain kind of future.

We create even more positive impact when we connect with people that have similar cares, and we form networks and teams to make and fulfill promises. Our purpose as Altus is to help people in companies and organizations lead and team in ways that produce both business results and people who feel alive, valued, and capable. This is our shared care. On our team, we each have distinctive cares that align with this in some way.

*We talk about our team not as
a group we "go to" but as a
home base we "come from."*

So, the first conversation we have with any person looking to join our team is this: What do you care about? How are you taking care of this care? How would joining the Altus team enable you to accomplish this even more fully?

Our clarity on these fundamental questions orients us to what we do together. This helps us make sure that working with the Altus team truly aligns with the future each person wants to build, so that working together becomes a source of energy, not depletion. We talk about our team not as a group we "go to" but as a home base we "come from."

From this shared base, we extend ourselves to take action in the world. Care guides us when we hit a roadblock or something just feels off. We come back to how we want to take care of our care and figure out how we can do that in this situation. Working this way, we're more satisfied, we're more motivated to make it through hard times together, and we brim with energy for our clients and their success.

We also act from care when we honor our colleagues for whom Altus is no longer a fit. We adapt to their changing reality, and we support them in the transition, while we check in with ourselves to make sure that we remain genuinely aligned as a team.

We declare and regularly re-commit to our future.

As we describe in this book, commitments give teams a powerful opportunity to create the future together. This is the second conversation we have with people who want to join Altus: What is the commitment that you will make as it relates to Altus?

We want our team members to make commitments that energize, drive, and fulfill them. We explore together how your commitment takes care of both the Altus promise to clients and your individual care. This further generates our sense of belonging while being successful together.

What's important here is that we ask team members to be clear about their commitment. Each member decides the scope of their commitment and how they will fulfill it. We're not looking for a specific time commitment, which is what most organizations expect: *I spend darn near all my time with you, so, I guess we're a team.* Instead, we ask for commitments to specific outcomes. To produce those outcomes, we don't ask team members to limit their work to a defined consulting toolkit. Instead, we ask team members to bring the best of their unique experiences and to co-create with each other and our clients.

At this point, it won't come as a surprise that each person on our team listens for commitments from each other. To support those commitments, we talk openly about where we are competent and not yet competent to fulfill these commitments. This openness means we can learn from each other and from missteps when they happen.

By making our commitments, competence, and stumbles visible, we learn from experience, give each other feedback, get better, and make new commitments. Our empathy for each other as competent performers who are also avid learners has been a great driver of our success as a team.

We lead and operate from our values, and we regularly revisit and question them.

How do we operate? What's allowed and not allowed? How do we support each other? What do we do when breakdowns arise? We answer these questions and many more by referring to the values we've crafted for our team.

We have determined four values to guide and sustain our Altus team: Abundance, Joy, Legitimacy, and Responsibility:

Abundance: *Seeing ample possibilities for Me, We, and the World*[80]
There are always more possibilities available than what's right in front of us. We work from abundance when we enter initial conversations with a business leader with no expectation that a contract will follow. Abundance is why we never take on a client just because they might pay well. Abundance guides us when we help others grow their careers in this work.

Joy: *Cultivating a mood of grateful aliveness*
We are talking about a mood rather than an emotion. You can be feeling sad, frustrated, angry, overwhelmed, etc. and still operate from a mood of joy. We are grateful to be working with each other, and we have fun. When we are in contact with our own joy, we can bring lightness to our clients—not to be goofy (though sometimes we are!), but to expand and celebrate the ways in which we overcome obstacles and create success together.

Legitimacy: *Honoring the humanity and voice of every person*
We are each different observers, have different trigger points, and bring different perspectives. We see this as a beautiful source of our success: We don't "accept" diversity; we welcome and include differences. We respect the fullness of people's histories, and we honor the perspective they bring. Legitimacy lives in how we listen. We are endlessly willing to be transformed by conversations with people in and beyond the team.

Responsibility: *Choosing to see and take action to fulfill the commitments we make as Altus*

> We make commitments in our team, and we take a posture of responsibility to all commitments we make. This is where I stand for the success of my teammates, and each of them stands for my success, as we collaborate on this commitment that we call Altus. With responsibility, we speak up when something is missing, we communicate to stay on the same page, and we make commitments that generate our future together.

We pay attention to moods as a source of information about what's missing. At any moment we each live in a particular mood. Our values identify the moods in which we want to be a team together. When we're in moods driven by our values—such as curiosity, ambition, and connection—we create amazing results.

When we notice ourselves or our teammates in moods that don't reflect our values—such as scarcity, resignation, or annoyance—we speak up. We bring awareness not to suppress those moods, but to explore them and find the missing conversations that bring us back to living our values.

Trust is the currency of any relationship, and this becomes even more important in a team.

We cultivate trust and create safe space to be vulnerable and rebuild trust.

Trust is the currency of any relationship, and this becomes even more important in a team. Teamwork requires extending trust and behaving in ways that are worthy of trust. So, we do the work to build trust, and at times we need to spend time *rebuilding* trust.

Sometimes, we step on each other's toes and make messes: An unexpected decision was made. A team member is no longer at ease with a course of action. Someone is overwhelmed. A team member's expertise in a certain area has not been clearly understood. We haven't communicated in ways that others understand what we intended, etc.

These are all situations that have occurred in the Altus team. Each one of them presented an opportunity to rebuild trust and even strengthen that trust. When we make missteps, we clean things up. We listen more deeply, we apologize in ways that honor each person's dignity, we make commitments to do better, and we show each other grace.

Business culture sometimes views sharing vulnerabilities as a sign of weakness. We've found that our willingness to be vulnerable produces a strong bond and deep connection. It provides a safe place where we can talk about mistakes and areas for learning without shame or blame. We don't need to hide breakdowns, put on false bravado, or point fingers. Because we choose to be vulnerable, we can stand for each other's success.

We are exploring the unknown together.

What we don't know is infinitely greater than that what we do know. How refreshing! From the space of not knowing comes innovation. Yet, at some edge, we all have a fear of stepping into the unknown.

This is no different at Altus. Working with clients at the leading edges of their industries raises all sorts of fears from time to time: fear of being seen as not fully competent in a certain area, fear of misunderstanding the client's situation, fear of inadvertently shaming a client or team member with a direct remark, and so on.

Recognizing the fear and the anxieties that come with the unknown is important, so no one feels alone. We make time for each other. We ask how each other is doing, and we listen to their answer. We make time to experiment and design new approaches together. As we come to see each other's strengths in action, we learn how to move through challenges as they arise. It's our never-ending practice to support each other as we step into something we don't know, to explore fresh possibilities for each other and our clients, and to trust that we will land on our feet together.

We learn from each other, and we help each other learn faster and more deeply.

At the age of 87, Michelangelo shared, "I am still learning." If this was true for one of the greatest artists of all time, it's definitely true for us as a team.

Love of learning is probably one of the factors that most unites us as a team. We share a sense of curiosity and a desire to challenge and be challenged. We're open to stepping into unknown domains. We're committed to revisiting what we already know, but from different perspectives. We're also available to unlearn things that we once held true, so we can make way for a new practice.

———————————

*Learning requires a dojo—
a place of both safety and challenge
where we each expand the boundaries
of what we can do masterfully.*

———————————

Learning requires a dojo—a place of both safety and challenge where we each expand the boundaries of what we can do masterfully. We've found a rhythm of conversations crucial to creating our team dojo, especially as a remote-first global consultancy. Our weekly meetings are alive with curiosity and celebration, as we share current initiatives and request input. Three times a year we gather in person (as much as possible) for deeper learning and designing the future. These periodic gatherings are so essential to our learning and collaboration—and so joyful—that we manage our calendars to be there. This isn't because an absence will remove us from the team or damage our reputations. We show up to our team dojo because this is where we grow together to fulfill our shared commitment to creating workplaces that work.

We are in a practice of practicing.

The more we practice together, the more we're able to produce value. We also notice that practicing our craft together increases our feelings of belonging and trust. So, we pay attention to how we do what we do to produce meaningful results. Our attention to practice allows us to fail, recommit, ask for help, choose better methods, and truly embody the learning. We're in this together.

Our team is no different from the soccer team referenced at the beginning of this book. The more we practice together, the better we get. We see that this is not common sense in the prevailing business culture. People are often rewarded for what they know—not necessarily for what they learn and become able to do consistently. By learning and practicing together, we serve as mirrors, guides, and champions for each other. We also become reliable in our ability to produce results together.

OH, AND WE ARE HUMAN BEINGS!

On our team, we get to show up as whole people. Beautiful, sensitive, smart, and sometimes annoying human beings. We have weaknesses and talents, we have skills and flaws, we have quirks and tendencies, we can be exuberant or frustrated, we have good days and bad days, we have blind spots and epiphanies . . . is this starting to look familiar?

On our team, we honor ourselves as human beings. Recognizing and acknowledging these elements is what produces trust. Ask yourself, have you ever trusted a "perfect" person? You might have been impressed, but did you really trust them? I sure haven't, as I knew I was always missing something. Here we recognize no one is perfect at everything. Our grace for each other and the way we stand for each other's learning lets us stay honest, close, and helpful.

The result: We've been able to take a group of competent solo practitioners and build a team that is succeeding in taking care of what we and our clients care about in ways that align with our values. It doesn't get better than that.

CLOSING:
YOUR MOVE

Kobe Bogaert and Pam Fox Rollin

A t the beginning of this book, we invited you on a journey to explore the pitfalls, promises, and practices of growing groups into teams. Now that you've been on this journey with us, how will you use these insights to make your team satisfying and successful—maybe even amazing?

In the first part of our journey, we shared our definitions of teams, how they differ from groups, and why this difference matters to the ambitions you and your organization can fulfill. As we've seen, people are used to being rewarded for their excellence as solo performers. Nearly everyone starts their career in this individual mindset, and many remain stuck there—even when they're operating in a group. Then, some people realize that investing effort in developing their team means they can even make bigger contributions and earn greater rewards. It takes choice, focus, and practice to move from maximizing individual success to building a team that can produce better outcomes. This holds true for executive teams as well as for teams throughout a company. We've also seen how mindset and practices of teams enable organizations and communities to accomplish more—even outside the formal bounds of team membership.

In the second section, we explored what you need to make teams great. Sometimes people assume being on a great team is a matter of luck: "We ended up with the right members!"

We encouraged you to focus instead on the actions that make teams great. Without these actions, it's unlikely the "right" members will coordinate well enough to produce their best results. You've seen how successful teams create and fulfill a shared promise.[81] They pay attention to how commitment to that promise lives in their conversations and relationships. Teams flourish when each member takes not only accountability for their tasks, but responsibility for the overall results and the full team's experience and growth.

In the third section, we focused on how you can build teams in our complex and diverse world. We showed how organizations make the most of diversity by more fully including a variety of voices. We've learned to slow down sometimes—to become curious about what else is available to see and to listen more effectively. We can then move faster, together, in a better direction. We also highlighted the central role played by trustworthy behavior, curiosity, and clear communication in successful hybrid and remote teams. Trust and inclusion are especially important when working across generational expectations, multiple time zones, and/or cultural differences. We showed the sort of conversations that build, sustain, and repair trust in diverse teams.

Finally, we looked at the role of the individual in building the team. How you lead directly impacts how successfully the team collaborates and supports each other. We shared the importance of vulnerability and reflection, as your self-awareness and growth as a person deepens the growth you can facilitate on your team. We described how to create the future by designing action with others instead of directing them to do the next task. We were also delighted to share what we do as an Altus team that allows us to produce exceptional results, have a blast working together, and become more capable every day. Your ability to evolve your workgroup into a team enables you to make bigger promises, produce better results, and develop people faster and more deeply.

Now that you've completed this journey, we invite you to see yourself as a leader committed to and capable of building and sustaining successful teams. Where you don't yet have capability, commit to learn. Your commitment sets into motion a virtuous cycle: When you take trustworthy actions to build a stronger team, then your team feels safer to learn, you all raise your competence, and you achieve more. As markets and opportunities change, welcoming diverse perspectives and your capacity to design together enables your team to adapt and thrive.

So, how will you use the insights you've gained to make your team amazing?

We suggest that you consider the following reflections:

- **Take a look at your current team(s).** How are you doing relative to the ten elements in the *Foundations* chapter? Observe, make a few notes, and invite your teammates to join you, first by identifying your shared promises, then working through each of the elements. Be excited about finding gaps— these become opportunities for your team to act and grow!

- **Assess yourself as a member and leader of teams.** Ask your team members how they can count on you, what works for them, and what could be improved. Be curious and grateful for their insights.

- **Look for opportunities for improvement.** As you are reflecting and listening, are you seeing new actions you can take to improve your team? Bring those insights to your team and invite them to co-design. Be open to experimenting and learning by designing, acting, and reflecting together.

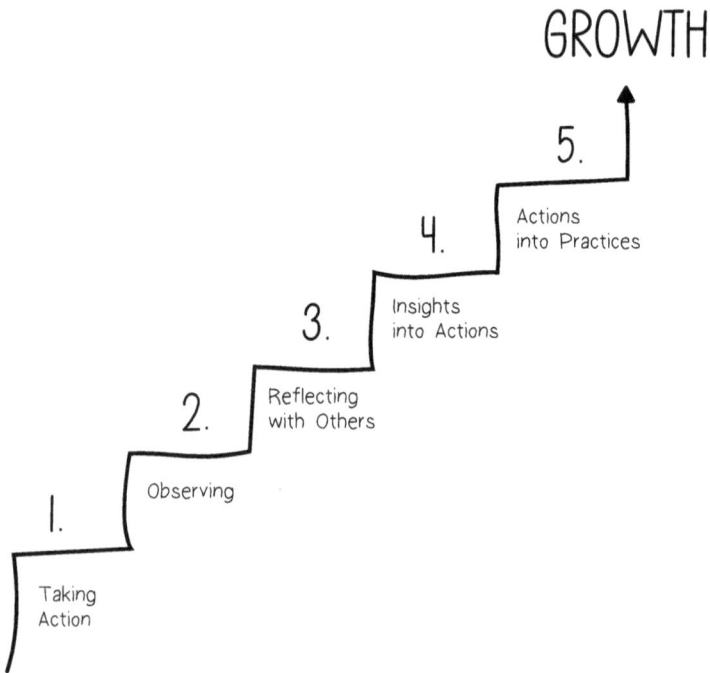

GROWTH

5.
Actions
into Practices

4.
Insights
into Actions

3.
Reflecting
with Others

2.
Observing

1.
Taking
Action

Growth comes from taking action, observing what happens, and reflecting with others on ways to improve—then, turning insights into actions and actions into practices. Sometimes you can get all the guidance you need within your team. Sometimes you and your teammates are so busy getting results and so accustomed to working in certain ways that you'd benefit from skilled external help. Good sports teams have coaches to help players (especially the stars!) see fresh possibilities, practice, adapt, and better coordinate with teammates. If you find yourself and your teams wanting to grow faster, address more complex opportunities, and make and fulfill bigger promises, we invite you to reach out to us for a conversation.

Finally, we want to remind you to be compassionate with yourself and your teams. They've brought you to where you are now. If you want to achieve more in a more satisfying way, you now have powerful ways to do this.

As you open conversations to strengthen your team, you're creating new levels of joy and results for you, your team, organization, customers, and communities.

Enjoy the journey!

APPENDICES

GROW YOUR COMPANY'S FUTURE WITH ALTUS

Altus Growth Partners is a global consulting and coaching firm working with leaders and teams to become more collaborative, effective, inclusive, and productive.

- Vision, Mission, & Strategy
- Effective Teams at All Levels
- Culture & Collaboration
- Operational Practices
- Executive Coaching & Leadership Development

See more at altusgrowth.com/how-we-help

At Altus, everything we do is based on the recognition that great accomplishments are driven by the genuine commitment and coordination of leaders, teams, and organizations. Where purpose and accountabilities are clear and strong, so are results and satisfaction.

Our care is about impacting leaders and teams to work more productively with each other and with the organization to drive measurable breakthroughs. We show leaders and teams how to have the conversations they need to build the strong culture that can address challenges and manage opportunities both now and in the future.

We work with leaders like you who are committed to growth, open to possibilities, and willing to enter in new conversations and practices on how to grow your people as well as the organization.

If you're aiming for bold change and growing your leadership, teams, and organization to create extraordinary results, we want to talk to you! Schedule your confidential conversation:

altusgrowth.com
altusconnect@altusgrowth.com

ALTUS GROWTH PARTNERS— OUR VALUES

Our success at Altus Growth Partners is guided by these values and key behaviors. We're sharing them here as an example of an actionable value statement that may be useful for your own team.

VALUES	KEY BEHAVIORS (What we expect to see from each other if we are living these values)
ABUNDANCE **Seeing ample possibilities for Me, We, and the World**	• We value our work as "illuminators" who deliver on commitments. • We accept engagements when clients are committed and ready. • We commit to work when we have capacity to meet our standards. • We staff projects with 2+ team members, and we help each other grow. • We keep our hearts and minds open to fresh possibilities.

LEGITIMACY **Honoring the** **humanity and** **voice of every** **person**	• We welcome and listen for differing views and diverse perspectives. • We invite our clients to honor the people and voices in their world. • We are caring mirrors and noble adversaries for each other and clients. • We speak our observations and assessments without shame or blame. • We are open to being transformed in conversation.
JOY **Cultivating a** **mood[82] of grateful** **aliveness**	• We express gratitude for and appreciation of each other and our clients. • We make space for playfulness and laughter in our conversations. • We notice, name, and explore when moods of contraction show up. • We offer joy as our practice and as a distinction in our work. • We celebrate individual and team successes and learnings.
RESPONSIBILITY **Choosing to see** **and take action** **to fulfill the** **commitments we** **make as Altus**	• I/We make trustworthy commitments for the future of our team, clients, and partners. • I/We take a posture of responsibility to all Altus commitments. • I/We navigate to stay on the same page with all our customers and performers. • I/We speak up when I/we see something is missing for achieving our commitment. • I/We make offers and extend help to fulfill the promise of the team. • I/We take a stand for the success of the people with whom I/we make commitments.

RESOURCES

BOOK SITE:
CONTINUE YOUR LEARNING ABOUT TEAMS

Our website includes an ever-growing set of case studies, articles, videos, assessments, and resources to help you build amazing teams.

altusgrowth.com/book

WE'D LOVE TO HEAR FROM YOU

- What are your most valuable takeaways or insights?

- What will you do differently because of what you read in this book?

- What questions do you have about teams?

Contact us at altusconnect@altusgrowth.com

PODCAST: LISTEN TO MISSING CONVERSATIONS

How do you create extraordinary and meaningful outcomes that take care of people, your organization, and the future you care about?

We at Altus believe all results—those that you want and those that you don't—are generated by conversations. When conversations are missing, people and results suffer. Learning to see the missing conversations is where to begin. Helping you and your teams have the right conversations with the right people to get the results you desire is what Altus is all about.

Through in-depth interviews with incredible guests, we explore the power and practices of conversations. In each interview, you'll learn how to see the missing conversations to enhance your leadership influence and impact and ignite a world of difference, one conversation at a time.

Listen to the Missing Conversations podcast on Apple Podcasts, Spotify, or the Altus Growth Partners website: **altusgrowth.com/podcast**

INSTITUTE FOR GENERATIVE LEADERSHIP: GROW YOUR FUTURE AS A LEADER AND COACH

Altus Growth Partners grew out of deep professional relationships forged through the Institute for Generative Leadership (IGL), and we are glad to recommend IGL as part of your development as a leader or organizational coach.

From IGL: At IGL, we believe we can create a world in which everyone thrives. The possibilities we want to create start in conversations. When we become clear on what matters most, we can engage in conversations about how to design the future we want.

Visit us for current programs at **generateleadership.com**.

INDEX

ACKNOWLEDGMENTS

This book is the result of inspiration from and trusted relationships with clients, teammates, teachers, our families, and our professional learning communities. We are grateful to the many heads, hands, and hearts which have contributed to this team effort to create this book to uplift teams. We extend special gratitude to these supporters of this book:

- The leaders and teams who have trusted us to work with them and learn. Your desire for better organizations inspires us, and you co-created everything we know how to do.

- Bob Dunham and the Institute for Generative Leadership community, for the rigorous program of leadership development and organizational excellence that deepened, nurtured, and connected us as professionals.

- The research and teachings of many before us, whose work articulated language as action, learning as embodied behavior, and choice as ever present: Bob Dunham, Julio Olalla, Dr. Fernando Flores, Dr. Richard Strozzi-Heckler, and many more.

- Linda Popky, for her editorial review, excellent advice, and critical guidance.

- Pamela Partington, for diverse and inspiring illustrations.

- Jeanne Schreiber and Holly Barimah, for help with graphical design and layout.
- Chalmers Brothers and Donice Alverson, for guidance on the text.
- Kobe Bogaert, for leading this catalyst-for-illumination that we call Altus.
- Pam Fox Rollin, for launching, shaping, and leading this book.
- Jan Irene Miller, for delving into the history of generative leadership to produce citations.
- Altus Growth Partners chapter authors—Amy Vodarek, Dan Winter, Heather Neely, Jan Irene Miller, Juliana Vergara, Steven Jones—and our contributing colleagues—Andrea Bordenca, Maribell Gonzalez, Sailaja Manacha, Sameer Dua, and Sheeja Shaju—for your writing, re-writing, and determination to give teams everywhere the gift of your experiences and insights through this book.
- Our Altus Growth Partners teammates who joined us in the course of the book and cheered every step, including Jon Osborne, Elayna Alexandra, Karuna Dera, and Lynette Winter.
- Our beloved colleague Marc Smith Sacks, an amazing team member whose time with us was cut short. Your delight in learning guides us more than you could know.
- Our teams at home. We feel your support!

ABOUT THE AUTHORS

Kobe Bogaert, MBA works with senior executives and leadership teams of private and public companies in the US and Europe. With his Altus Growth Partners team, Kobe guides technology, biotech, distribution, manufacturing, and professional service companies through strategy development, executive team development, high stakes conflict resolution, leadership development, organizational culture, and business process development. Kobe's ability to question client assumptions allows them to experience extraordinary growth for themselves, their teams, and their organizations.

Pam Fox Rollin, MBA coaches senior executives and top teams in Silicon Valley and globally. Pam guides technology, biopharma, and healthcare organizations to succeed in strategic transformation, executive development, acquisition integration, and culture change. Her book, *42 Rules for Your New Leadership Role*, is described as an indispensable guide for leaders at all levels. Pam loves to make a difference where highly capable people are thinking through their most consequential strategic and organizational opportunities.

Amy Vodarek, MScN, PCC, NCC coaches executives, senior leaders, and founders in healthcare, health technology, and social impact sectors. Amy helps clients align their strategic initiatives to advance their vision. She also guides women executives and founders to expand their effectiveness and impact as host of *The Feminine Edge* Podcast and co-author of *Good Enough: Embrace who you are. Unleash Your Brilliance.* Amy is passionate about helping visionary women leaders leverage their unique strengths and advance their bold ideas for change.

Andrea Bordenca is an entrepreneur, executive coach, and youth and adult leadership educator. Andrea serves as Managing Partner of Generative Consulting, CEO and chairperson of DESCO Service, founder of Lead Yourself Youth, principal of Venture Way Collaborative, and co-founder of The Women's Collaborative. Andrea thrives when people of all ages, races, and genders are in dialogue together. She believes that the only way toward systemic change is by bringing all community stakeholders together to create change together.

Dan Winter, MBA, MS works with successful leaders around the world facing their most challenging situations to generate fresh insights and innovative approaches to reach new levels of results. His diverse, international clients have leveraged his deep expertise in coaching, team and organization development, strategy, and culture change to thrive in dynamic markets and create high-performing, inclusive cultures as they capitalize on global opportunities.

Heather Neely, MA partners with senior executives and teams across the globe in biotech, high tech, and the entertainment industry with one mission in mind: to help people and organizations produce desired results. There is an art and science to generating high performance, and Heather is passionate about revealing the mystery of effective actions in teams and systems. Heather's approach allows leaders to access their strengths, build effective relationships on teams, speak powerfully, and take appropriate action.

Jan Irene Miller, MBA coaches executive teams as they focus on strategic transformation and self-development to create powerful leaders of the future. Her twenty years growing and managing global professional service technology teams have shaped her abilities to support diverse, dispersed teams of professionals. Jan Irene is an artist, certified somatic and executive coach, coach supervisor, and steward of her 220-acre woodlands, offering a place for learning and connecting with nature and all that sustains life.

Juliana Vergara, PCC, MS Clinical Psychology coaches senior and emerging leaders in both the United States and Latin America. Her passion for leadership development and intentional growth has led her to impact the careers and lives of the people she coaches. Juliana's clients have experienced significant transformation, based on better understanding of themselves, who they lead, and what matters to them. She deeply cares about creating a world where people play bigger games without sacrificing their well-being.

Maribell González, PCC is an entrepreneur, executive coach and consultant, and coach educator. She serves as CEO of the Institute for Generative Leadership for Latin America, leading teams and projects in more than 12 countries. Maribell helps leaders create safe spaces that help them and their teams to free their potential and create new results with dignity and belonging. She is also passionate about guiding teams and individuals in finding their purpose and healing relationships and conversations to create healthy cultures.

Sailaja Manacha, TSTA (Psychotherapy), PCC coaches senior executives in India and globally. Her clients include technology and healthcare companies, where she facilitates leaders to hone their relational intelligence for impact and influence with their teams and key stakeholders. She has a special focus on the growth of women leaders, and her book *Step Up* was a #1 best seller on Amazon. Sai is passionate about leaders and teams reaching their goals through self-mastery and productive relationships.

Sameer Dua, MCom recognized amongst the top 30 emerging thinkers of the world by Thinkers50, is a best-selling author, a coach for leading coaches and global business leaders, founder of the London Business Literature Festival and the Gift Your Organ Foundation, and has over 30 years' experience in management and leadership education. Sameer is the CEO of the Institute for Generative Leadership (UK and Asia) and previously ran management institutes in six cities of India and the UK, with students from 52 different countries.

Sheeja Shaju, MS guides corporate executives, business owners, and emerging talent to make and deliver bigger promises through her company, I Create. For eight years, Sheeja led programs and coached for Institute for Generative Leadership-Asia, and worked as Director of Learning and Somatics. She has 25 years of experience as a coach and trainer in such companies as Hershey, Cummins, Siemens, BMC Software, Mercedes Benz, and Kohler.

Steven E. Jones, PhD is an executive coach, advisor, and consultant who works with US and international leaders. Steven inspires and guides leaders across systems to navigate cultural transformation. He partners with executives and their teams to build organizational cultures that increase value, improve lives, and expand the capacity of communities to achieve outcomes that transform challenges into opportunities. Steven merges wisdom, care, results-based leadership, and generative distinctions to engage the whole person in building practices to thrive.

NOTES

INTRODUCTION

1. Gallup, Inc., "State of the Global Workplace 2023 Report," Gallup.com, copyright 2023, https://www.gallup.com/workplace/349484/state-of-the-global-workplace-report.aspx

2. Ibid.

3. "Leadership in Today's Society," Simon Sinek, October 15, 2018, https://simonsinek.com/discover/putting-others-first/.

WELCOME

4. Deloitte 2019 Global Capital Trends, "Leading the social enterprise: Reinvent with a human focus," April 2019, 53–66, https://www2.deloitte.com/content/dam/insights/us/articles/5136_HC-Trends-2019/DI_HC-Trends-2019.pdf.

5. The Ken Blanchard Companies, "High Performance Teams: What It Takes to Make Them Work," 2019, 2, http://www.blanchard.com.tr/Uploads/files/Arastirma/high-performance-teams-what-it-takes-to-make-them-work.pdf.

6. Group comes from Italian *gruppo*, "knot," which is thought to come from Proto-Germanic kruppaz, s.v. "group (n.)," *Online Etymology Dictionary*, https://www.etymonline.com/search?q=group&ref=searchbar_searchhint.

FOUNDATIONS

7. Bob Dunham, Institute for Generative Leadership, "Notes on Building and Leading Teams," (2008, 2017).

8. Peter J. Denning and Robert Dunham, *The Innovator's Way: Essential Practices for Successful Innovation* (Cambridge, MA: The MIT Press, 2010), 20. "The word *breakdown* is used by linguistics scholars for any event that interrupts the flow of action toward the desired outcome."

9. Alan Sieler, *Coaching to the Human Soul Ontological Coaching and Deep Change*, vol. 1 (Newfield: Australia, 2005), 317–347.

10. Chalmers Brothers and Vinay Kumar, *Language and the Pursuit of Leadership Excellence: How Extraordinary Leaders Build Relationships, Shape Culture and Drive Breakthrough Results*, 2nd ed. (Naples, FL: New Possibilities Press, 2015), 35.

11. Dunham, "Notes on Building and Leading Teams." Author's note: Bob Dunham showed us that teams are generated by conversations. The table distinctions are my own selection inspired by Bob Dunham's conversations of teams' framework. He also gave us the language to refer to a non-team as a group.

12. Brothers and Kumar, *Language and Leadership*, 37.

13. J. L. Austin, *How To Do Things With Words*, 2nd ed.: *The William James Lectures delivered at Harvard University* 1955, ed. J. O. Urmson and Marina Sbisà (Cambridge, MA: Harvard University Press, 4th Printing, 1981).

14. Fernanco Flores, Maria Flores Letelier ed., *Conversations for Action and Collected Essays*, (South Carolina: CreateSpace, 2012), Preface and Acknowledgements.

15. John R. Searle, *Speech Acts: An Essay in the Philosophy of Language*, (Cambridge University Press, 1969).

16. Meghan French Dunbar, "Designer Eileen Fisher on How Finding Purpose Changed Her Company," *SOCAPDIGITAL* online, July 2015, https://socapglobal.com/2015/07/designer-eileen-fisher-on-how-finding-purpose-changed-her-company/.

17. Naina Dhingra and Bill Schaninger, "The search for purpose at work," *McKinsey & Company: People & Organizational Performance* online, June 3, 2021, podcast , https://www.mckinsey.com/business-functions/people-and-organizational-performance/our-insights/the-search-for-purpose-at-work.

18. Bob Dunham, "Care, the Heart of Action, Meaning and Value," (Excellence in Generative Leadership program materials, 2016).

19. Figure 1. Robert Dunham, "The Generative Foundations of Action in Organizations: Speaking and Listening," *International Journal of Coaching in Organizations*, 2009 7(2),43-63.

20. Robert Dunham, "Me-We-World," Foundations of Generative Leadership Program (program handout and video recordings, Institute for Generative Leadership, 2017).

21. What makes teams successful? What Google's Project Aristotle concluded," *New Age Leadership* online, accessed 12/23/2021, https://newageleadership.com/what-makes-teams-successful-googles-project-aristotle-came-up-with-these-five-factors-that-matter/.

22. Amy C. Edmondson, *The Fearless Organization: Creating Psychological Safety in the Workplace for Learning, Innovation, and Growth* (Hoboken, NJ: Wiley, 2018).

23. Bob Dunham, "Emotions, Moods, and Action in Leadership," (program paper, Institute for Generative Leadership, 2019).

24. Flores, Letelier ed., *Conversations For Action and Collected Essays*, xiv.

25. Bob Dunham and Sameer Dua, *The Power of Owning Up: A Book on Responsibility for Leaders and Coaches* (India: Generative Leadership Publishing, 2022).

SECTION ONE

26. Bob Dunham, conversation with Institute for Generative Leadership program coaches, 2023.

27. "The Prisoner's Dilemma in Business and the Economy," Investopedia, accessed January 11, 2023, https://www.investopedia.com/articles/investing/110513/utilizing-prisoners-dilemma-business-and-economy.asp. William Poundstone, *Prisoner's Dilemma* (New York: Doubleday, 1992). Game theory was embraced at the RAND Corporation, the think tank charged with formulating military strategy for the atomic age. In 1950, two RAND scientists discovered the *prisoner's dilemma*—a disturbing game where two or more people may betray the common good for individual gain.

28. Leo Tolstoy, *Anna Karenina* (New York: Charles Scribner's Sons, 1922) "All happy families are alike; each unhappy family is unhappy in its own way."

29. Wageman et al. *Senior Leadership Teams: What It Takes to Make Them Great*, Canadian ed. (Boston, MA: Harvard Business Review Press, 2008).

30. Dunham, "Notes on Building and Leading Teams."

31. Denning and Dunham, *The Innovator's Way*, 20.

32. Dunham, "Notes on Building and Leading Teams."

33. Board members who come from investment backgrounds may have little experience building high-performance operating teams.

34. Dunham, "Care."

35. Flores, Letelier ed., *Conversations For Action and Collected Essays*, 27.

36. Bob Dunham, Institute for Generative Leadership, "Reporting on a Promise," 1999, 2009. Course materials

37. Bob Dunham, Institute for Generative Leadership, "Managing Breakdowns," 1999, 2009. Course materials

38. Bob Dunham, Enterprise Performance, "Interdependency Management Practices," 2005. Course materials

39. Everett M. Rogers, *Diffusion of Innovations*, 5th ed. (New York: Free Press, 2003).

40. Dunham, "Care."

41. Richard Strozzi-Heckler, *The Leadership Dojo: Build Your Foundation as an Exemplary Leader* (Berkeley, CA: Frog Books, 2007).

42. Assessments and expert opinions are not true or false. They are statements of judgment backed up—"grounded"—with observable facts.

43. Bob Dunham, Institute for Generative Leadership, Generative Leadership Program, "Introduction to the core competencies of management" (Business Design Associates), 1990.

44. Julio Olalla and Rafael Echeverría, Newfield Network, "Mastering the Art of Professional Coaching" program, 1994.

SECTION TWO

45. Flores, Letelier ed., *Conversations For Action and Collected Essays*, 31–33.

46. Dunham, "Notes on Building and Leading Teams."

47. Linguistic "acts" are the 1950s research and publication works of Oxford philosopher J. L. Austin and were later developed by University of California philosophy professor John Searle. Searle's student Dr. Fernando Flores and his company, Action Technology, brought "Speech Act Theory" into the field of management and leadership consulting.

48. Sameer Dua, *Become* (India: Harper Business, 2017).

49. Flores, Letelier ed., *Conversations For Action and Collected Essays*, 15.

50. Dunham and Dua, *Power of Owning Up*, 34.

51. Flores, Letelier ed., *Conversations For Action and Collected Essays*, 33.

52. Ibid, 31.

53. Dunham and Dua. *The Power of Owning Up*, 61.

54. Ibid.

55. Bob Dunham, Institute for Generative Leadership, program material with additions by Pam Fox Rollin and Amy Vodarek.

56. Gallup, Inc., "State of the American Manager Report," Gallup.com, 2015, https://www.gallup.com/services/182216/state-american-manager-report.aspx.

57. Erskine, R. G., Moursund, J. P., and Trautmann, R. L., *Beyond Empathy: A Therapy of Contact-in-Relationship.* (Philadelphia: Brunner/Mazel, 1999).

58. Gallup, "State of the American Manager."

59. Edmondson, *The Fearless Organization*.

60. Michael Schneider, "Google Spent 2 Years Studying 180 Teams. The Most Successful Ones Shared These 5 Traits," Inc.com, July 19, 2017, https://www.inc.com/michael-schneider/google-thought-they-knew-how-to-create-the-perfect.html.

61. Richard Strozzi-Heckler, *The Art of Somatic Coaching: Embodying Skillful Action, Wisdom, and Compassion*, Illustrated ed. (Berkeley, California: North Atlantic Books, 2014), 61, 149.

62. Gallup, "State of the American Manager."

63. Strozzi-Heckler, *The Leadership Dojo*, 85–86.

SECTION THREE

64. Laura Morgan Roberts, Anthony J. Mayo, and David A. Thomas, *Race, Work, and Leadership: New Perspectives on the Black Experience*, 1st ed. (Boston, MA: Harvard Business Review Press, 2019), 318–320.

65. David Rock and Heidi Grant, "Why Diverse Teams Are Smarter," *Harvard Business Review*, November 4, 2016, https://hbr.org/2016/11/why-diverse-teams-are-smarter.

66. Brothers and Kumar, *Language and Leadership*, 14. The OAR model was initially developed by Chris Argyris and Robert Putnam. Maribell Gonzalez, Global Institute for Generative Leadership, LATAM, further expanded the model adding an "A" for actor: the ability to observe newly, take new actions, and embody new skills.

67. Dunham, "Care."

68. Dunham, "Emotions, Moods, and Action in Leadership."

69. Dunham, "Me-We-World."

70. "Guillermo Wechsler: On Linguistic Games," (blog), accessed January 6, 2022, https://guillermowechsler.typepad.com/my_weblog/2007/04/on_linguistic_g.html. The distinctions of games were developed by Dr. Fernando Flores. The distinction here is drawn from the blog of Guillermo Wechsler. We can interpret many of our social practices as linguistic games—recurrent structures for coordinating action that have been developed over time, often through the natural evolution of action and practices rather than design.

71. Glenn E. Singleton, *Courageous Conversations about Race*, 3rd ed. (Dallas, TX: Corwin, 2021), 60. "To be anti-racist is to be active. Simply claiming to be non-racist and 'not see race in others' passively allows racism to continue."

72. Heather Nealy was a researcher for this book: Carolyn A. Martin and Bruce Tulgan, *Managing the Generation Mix: From Urgency to Opportunity*, 2nd ed. (Amherst, MA: H R D Press, 2006).

73. William & Neil Howe Strauss, *GENERATIONS The History of America's Future 1584 to 2069*, 1st ed. (New York: William Morrow & Co, 1991).

74. Brothers and Kumar, *Language and Leadership*, xiv.

SECTION FOUR

75. Bessel van der Kolk, MD, "The Body Keeps the Score: *Brain, Mind, and Body in the Healing of Trauma*, (New York: Viking, 2014), 46.

76. Strozzi-Heckler, *Somatic Coaching*, 46.

77. Van der Kolk, *Body Keeps the Score*.

78. Roderick Gilkey and Clint Kilts, "Cognitive Fitness," *Harvard Business Review*, November 1, 2007, https://hbr.org/2007/11/cognitive-fitness.

79. Dunham, "Care."

80. Dunham, "Me-We-World."

81. Dunham, "Notes on Building and Leading Teams."

APPENDICES

82. Note we are talking about joy as a mood rather than an emotion. You can be feeling sad, frustrated, angry, overwhelmed, etc. and still operate from a mood of joy.

www.ingramcontent.com/pod-product-compliance
Lightning Source LLC
Chambersburg PA
CBHW040914210326
41597CB00030B/5082